KU-610-167

MANAGING

Graeme Salaman

Open University Press
Buckingham · Philadelphia

Open University Press
Celtic Court
22 Ballmoor
Buckingham
MK18 1XW

and
1900 Frost Road, Suite 101
Bristol, PA 19007, USA

First Published 1995

Copyright © Graeme Salaman 1995

All rights reserved. Except for the quotation of short passages for the
purpose of criticism and review, no part of this publication may be
reproduced, stored in a retrieval system, or transmitted, in any form or
by any means, electronic, mechanical, photocopying, recording or
otherwise, without the prior written permission of the publisher or a
licence from the Copyright Licensing Agency Limited. Details of such
licences (for reprographic reproduction) may be obtained from the
Copyright Licensing Agency Ltd of 90 Tottenham Court Road, London,
W1P 9HE.

A catalogue record of this book is available from the British Library

ISBN   0 335 19363 3 (pb)   0 335 19364 1 (hb)

Library of Congress Cataloging-in-Publication Data
Salaman, Graeme.
    Managing/by Salaman Graeme.
        p.   cm. – (Managing work and organizations series)
    Includes bibliographical references and index.
    ISBN 0–335–19364–1   ISBN 0–335–19363–3 (pbk.)
    1. Management.   I. Title.   II. Series.
HD31.S26   1995
658 – dc20   94–26581
                                                                      CIP

Typeset by Type Study, Scarborough
Printed in Great Britain by St Edmundsbury Press Ltd,
Bury St Edmunds, Suffolk

Books are to be returned on or before
the last date below.

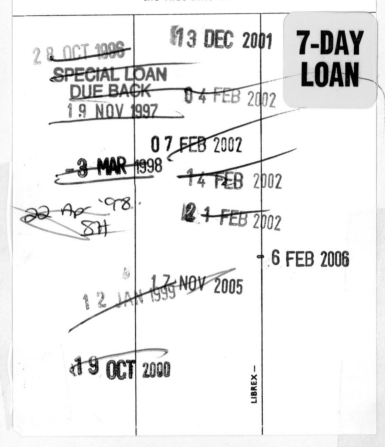

2 8 OCT 1996

13 DEC 2001

**7-DAY
LOAN**

SPECIAL LOAN
DUE BACK
1 9 NOV 1997

0 4 FEB 2002

0 7 FEB 2002

-3 MAR 1998

1 4 FEB 2002

22 Ap '978.
8H

2 1 FEB 2002

- 6 FEB 2006

1 2 JAN 1999

1 7 NOV 2005

1 9 OCT 2000

LIBREX —

LIVERPOOL JMU LIBRARY

3 1111 00660 5529

LIVERPOOL
JOHN MOORES UNIVERSITY
TRUEMAN STREET LIBRARY
15-21 WEBSTER STREET
LIVERPOOL L3 2ET
TEL 051 231 4022/4023

MANAGING WORK AND ORGANIZATIONS SERIES

Edited by Graeme Salaman, Reader in Sociology in the Faculty of Social Sciences and the Open Business School, the Open University

Current and forthcoming titles include:

For the three who matter most:
Rena, Alexandra and Sophie; this, and everything else.

CONTENTS

ACKNOWLEDGEMENTS

This book is the result of many, many hours of discussion over many years with many colleagues and friends. It is common for authors to preface their book with thanks to influential and helpful friends and associates. This convention is absolutely necessary in this case. In a real sense, the thinking outlined here is collaborative; the friends listed below contributed enormously. Even though they may not always know that they have contributed, or how or what they have contributed, I suspect that many will recognize familiar arguments or be able to recall conversations, some many years ago. I hope that the book does justice to their ideas.

I wish to thank and acknowledge the value of discussions on the topic of management, organization and learning with: Stephen Adler, Chris Argyris, David Ashton, Julian Batsleer, Jim Butler, David Casey, Tim Clark, Bill Critchley, Fiona Davidson, Paul du Gay, Kathryn Evans, Peter Honey, Paul Iles, Robin Jacobs, David Lloyd, Chris Mabey, Mary Mather, Alan Mumford, David Pearce, Steve Percy, Dhamika Premarathna, Steve Schneider, Maurice Saias, Rosie Thomson, Brian Woodall, and my friends in the TPLF, especially Seeye Arbraha, Teklewoini Assefa, and Yohanes Oqubay. Most of all, I want to thank and acknowledge the contribution of two close friends, staunch colleagues and occasional comrades in arms: Graham Mole and Roger Plant.

1

INTRODUCTION

This book[1] is an attempt to clarify the nature of the management role in today's organizations, and the skills and attributes that managers need in order to play their role properly. This essential starting point for any analysis of management skills has often been obscured; yet no analysis of how managers should manage is possible without a clear and well-based view of what managers are supposed to do.

Managers do a large number of different things. As senior, powerful members of employing organizations they have various demanding responsibilities. For example, very senior managers have the job of deciding what business is to be pursued – what goods and services offered to what sorts of clients in what areas. Senior managers also have the responsibility (one hopes) for building and ensuring the adequacy of the organization's capability – its structures and systems. However, this book is not about these managerial responsibilities, crucial as they are. For the purposes of this book a distinction is proposed between three areas of managerial activity:

- specialist, functional or technical expertise, such as quantity surveying, marketing, production, insurance broking, human resources, accountancy;

1

- commercial responsibility for achieving business targets, containing costs, building new business, etc.;
- straight management – i.e. responsibility for the work of others.

Any individual manager may have all three types of responsibility; but for the purposes of this book we are concerned only with the third: the manager's essentially *managerial* responsibilities – getting work done with and through others. Nevertheless, the fact that managers have all three sorts of responsibility, and that these activities require different skills, habits of behaviour and even mind-sets, is significant for an analysis of the skills of management, and this will contribute to the analysis of why managers sometimes choose to manage in ways that are inappropriate – by using non-managerial skills in management activities.

This book is about what it means to manage, what is required in achieving effective management and why many managers will find management difficult. The book is based on the conviction that many managers, when they manage other people, literally do not know what they are doing. This is not surprising – not because no one has told them what to do, but because too many people have told them what to do, and how to do it. Managers are swamped with advice, much of it sensible but much also pulling in different directions. The trouble with this advice, and the reason why I have risked adding to it, is that it over-complicates the essence of management by offering too many bullet-pointed lists of activities and responsibilities. Managing well is certainly complex and difficult, as will be seen; but the nature of management itself – the essentially management tasks – is surprisingly straightforward. What is required, and what this book attempts, is to identify the essential activities and responsibilities of management.[2]

Such an objective has probably never been more necessary and important. The nature of management – the roles managers are required to fulfil, the objectives they are expected to pursue, the skills (or, these days, the competences) they are seen to require, the attributes and personalities ('management style') they are seen to need – has always varied with conceptions of how organizations work. The manager under Taylorism or human

2

relations management was defined in specific and cha
(and different) ways. With current programmes of orga
change inspired by human resource strategies the m.......... is
seen as central to the achievement of organizational effectiveness
to a degree greater than ever before; and the critical skills and
competences of managers are defined more ambitiously than
previously. For example:

> Senior managers have been re-engineering business pro-
> cesses with a passion, tearing down corporate structures that
> no longer can support the organisation. Yet the practice of
> management has largely escaped demolition. If their jobs
> and styles are left largely intact, managers will eventually
> undermine the very structure of their rebuilt enterprises.
> The work of managers in a re-engineered organisation must
> change as much as the work of workers.
>
> (Champy, 1994: 17)

Yet while current conditions undoubtedly place new and
stronger pressures on managers, and have very definite implications for management style, the essence of management
remains the same as ever, and is actually quite simple and
straightforward (although difficult to achieve in practice). It is
this: managers only exist in order to enhance the quality of their
subordinates' work. If a manager is removed and the work of the
subordinates remains the same, over a substantial period, then
this must raise doubts about the necessity for, or competence of,
the absent manager. The writer quoted earlier seems to agree
with this. The words are different, more fashionable, but the
meaning is the same:

> The role of managers becomes one of empowerment –
> providing workers with the information, training, authority
> and accountability to excel in a re-engineered business
> process . . . managers . . . must inspect the work, measure
> the performance of the process and its contributors, and
> coach the workers to ever better performance.
>
> (Champy, 1994: 17)

From this it also follows that an indicator of a manager's
competence is the quality of performance of the manager's

subordinates. If the subordinates are failing, the manager is failing, for it is the manager's responsibility to work with subordinates to ensure that their performance is appropriate and adequate. Admittedly this is a very stark and demanding criterion by which to evaluate a manager's work. But how could there be any other? And if it is the job of managers to improve their subordinates' performance, then how can this be done? How can managers help or encourage or inspire others to do better? It is easy enough to assert that this is managers' responsibility, but another thing to be able to achieve it.

_ This performance focus of management is even more crucial under the programmes of rapid and fundamental change that are currently sweeping through organizations. For whatever the specific focus of these changes, they will certainly fail unless and until they are translated into the everyday behaviour of managers seeking to direct, encourage and enhance the work of their subordinates. All programmes of organizational change are ultimately programmes of management change, and rely totally on the managers concerned being able and willing to translate the overall vision and direction of change into the behaviour and attitudes of themselves and their staff. _

However, in practice managers spend their time in a great variety of activities, and seem to spend relatively little time on the activities we identify as the essence of management. Is this simply because they are confused by the plethora of advice on how to manage, or is there a deeper reason? There is another — reason – that to some extent managers tend to avoid addressing issues of the performance of their subordinates because they find this inherently difficult and awkward. Furthermore, these difficulties are not accidental – they arise from the managers' backgrounds, preferences and habits. Most managers are promoted to management because they are good at something else – something other than management. But these earlier skills are actually an *obstacle* to the development of management skills. Management skills are not simply different from the specialist, technical or discipline skills of the manager, but in some cases and some senses *opposed* to them.

But it is still possible to overcome barriers of habit and ingrained ways of thinking and behaving, and to develop the necessary skills of management as defined in this book. Such a process of development starts with the recognition of what management is essentially about, but then proceeds to the key tasks of management – the skills of helping others learn and improve. The second half of this book is dedicated to understanding how people (managers) can help others do what they do better, or to do better things. This requires a consideration of how people learn, and how the behaviour of other people who want us to improve can help or hinder that process.

The book is organized as follows. First, there is a consideration of current developments in organizations and in their environments which make the role and the successful achievement of effective management ever more critical to organizational success. The following chapter considers what managers actually *do*, how they actually spend their time. If we are to be able to develop a model of how managers *should* behave in order to manage well, and if we are to assist the development of the skills we identify as critical, it is necessary to have some information on how they actually spend their time. This chapter lays the foundations for the later analysis of key management skills.

Next, there is a more conceptual analysis of the manager's role. This takes us away from what managers *actually* do, and begins an analysis of what they *should* do. It involves a move from the descriptive to the conceptual – to what they should do if they are to achieve the requirements of the role. In the light of this analysis of the manager's role, the following chapters consider the skills that managers will need to do what they should do – to manage well. This discussion begins with a consideration of recent work on managerial competences. Chapter 4 discusses and evaluates some key contributions to, and developments within, the competence approach to the identification of the qualities necessary for effective management. The competence approach is important and interesting. It deserves attention if only for its claim to offer a breakthrough in the discussion of management.

However, the key managerial competences as described in this book are those which support the management of performance, or the management of learning, for this is seen as the key activity of managers *qua* managers. This view is explained and justified in Chapters 5 and 6. Chapter 5 offers a view of the main elements of the management role, and Chapter 6 presents the book's view of the core management activities and skills.

Chapter 7 considers how learning – that is, performance improvement – can be achieved. And Chapters 8 and 9 consider the relationship between organizations and learning. Chapter 8 discusses barriers to learning within organizations, and Chapter 9, taking a more positive stance, discusses the learning organization – how organizational structures can actually encourage learning.

Chapter 10 takes a more practical approach and considers how managers can encourage the learning of others. The focus here is on the key prerequisite skills or understandings which the management of performance requires, through a consideration of the role of management styles. Achieving the appropriate style of management is critical to successful management as defined in this book. Also, the importance of achieving the appropriate type of relationship with, or approach to, the manager's subordinates (or colleagues) is fundamental, and this issue is explored through consideration of a useful model of approaches to relationships called transactional analysis.

Finally, Chapter 11 offers some suggestions for practical exercises which could be used to develop the approach presented in the book.

Notes

1 The financial support of the ESRC (grant no. R000234869) is gratefully acknowledged.
2 This book will not cover training issues that arise from the analysis of the management role and core management skills. The analysis of relevant training would fill a book in itself. Clearly, the view of management presented in the book has major implications for the design of training in management skills. Some of the issues raised have been briefly covered elsewhere (Mole *et al.*, 1993).

2

THE ROLE OF
MANAGEMENT SKILLS IN
TODAY'S ORGANIZATIONS

Managerial leadership in large corporations is . . . facing complex issues that require not only decisiveness but creativity; not only managerial control but visionary leadership; not only the technical skills necessary to achieve the organisation's mission but the integrity to resolve the value conflicts inherent in shaping that mission.

(Kolb *et al.*, 1986: 13)

Management skills have always been important, but their importance has recently grown enormously as a result of two developments: an increased awareness of the importance of management as a key to competitive advantage, and an increased burden of responsibility being placed on management as a result of current organizational changes.

Organizations are currently facing increasingly difficult and demanding environmental conditions: increased competitive pressure, global competition often from Japan and the Far East; deregulation in many sectors, technological change, increased legal and environmental pressure-group demands, more differentiated and demanding markets. Frequently reactions to these pressures take the form of some restructuring of key organizational dimensions.

For example, Storey and Sisson (1993: 19) argue that using 25 key human resource variables to examine the extent of take-up of human resource management (HRM), when applied to 15 mainstream companies, showed

> extensive take-up of HRM style approaches in the British mainstream organizations. Two-thirds of the companies recorded a definite tick scoring on at least 11 of the dimensions . . . Such has been the apparent level of engagement with these new sets of beliefs values and practices that the evidence points to a wholescale shift away from the proceduralist recipe in our major employing organizations.

Their results are included in Table 2.1.

~ The term 'proceduralist' refers to the now largely discredited idea that procedures, rules and formalized arrangements are the best method for ensuring that staff behave appropriately. The emphasis now, as the table suggests, is on reducing constraints and controls in order to 'liberate' the innate capacities of the individual, and to encourage initiative and entrepreneurship. This shift places far greater reliance on the responsibilities and capacities of managers. Storey and Sisson support this view that current changes – and current talk about the desirability of organizational change – place new and great emphasis on the role of manager:

> the case studies uniformly revealed the impressive emergence of 'general business managers' and line managers as key players on employment issues. In all 15 cases there was evidence of these managers devising, driving and delivering new initiatives . . . line managers as well as personnel directors were intent on stressing their engagement with 'culture change' activities.
>
> (Storey and Sisson, 1993: 23)

A study sponsored by the Foundation for Management Education and Ashridge Management College, argues 'that organizations of the future will form a different context for the practice of management: a context in which flexibility and commitment will be key attributes within the decentralized but strongly integrated organization' (Barham *et al.*, 1988: 37).

⌐ Various management writers and consultants have argued that for organizations to survive under these demanding conditions, radical change is necessary, and, furthermore, that it is occurring (Thomson *et al.*, 1985; Pettigrew, 1988). Central to this process of organizational restructuring is what is known as human resource management (HRM) or human resource strategies (HRS). ⌐

⌐Conceptions of the necessary features of the manager – and, indeed, of what management itself means – have varied over the recent history of the development of work organizations. The manager has always been a contingent element of theories of organization. In his classic analysis of managerial activity and authority, Bendix (1956), for example, notes that ideas used to legitimate management authority vary with historical period. More significantly from our view point, philosophies of organization (and specifically of work design) have carried major implications for the definition of the tasks of manager.

⌐ Taylorism, for example, essentially invented management as we know it. Under Taylorism, the manager not only took responsibilities and skills previously the property of workers, but also systematically took responsibility for taking these responsibilities. Thus, for example, the manager's job was to assemble all of the great mass of traditional knowledge, which had previously been in the heads of the workmen. Taylor was adamant that scientific management was more to do with the manager than with the worker. If the workers' job was transformed, so to a greater degree was the manager's. Since the manager now had to study the workers, design work to ensure maximum productivity, assess the workers' qualities and ensure that workers were in the right jobs for their abilities, ⌐

> there is no end to the things that you [the manager] may thus find which, if you think about them rightly, you will conclude that it is really your part of the business as a true manager to have looked after in a careful and systematic manner, in order to get the most out of your machines and their attendants.
>
> (Taylor, quoted in Bendix, 1956: 272)

Taylor noted that managers resisted their new (managerial) responsibilities: '. . . nine tenths of our trouble has been to

Table 2.1 Take-up of human resource management in British companies

	Austin Rover	British Rail	Bradford Council	Eaton Ltd	Ford	ICI	Jaguar	Lucas	Massey Ferguson	NHS	Peugot-Talbot	Plessey	Rolls-Royce	Smith & Nephew	Whitbread	
Beliefs and assumptions																
'Business need' is prime guide to action	✓	✓	✓	●	✓	✓	✓	✓	✓	●	✓	✓	✓	✓	✓	13
Aim to go 'beyond contract'	✓	●	✓	✓	✓	✓	✓	✓	✓	✓	●	✓	●	●	✓	11
Values/mission	✓	●	✓	✓	✓	✓	✓	✓	✓	✓	✓	●	●	●	✓	11
Impatience with rules	✓	●	✓	✓	●	✓	✓	✓	✓	✓	✓	●	●	●	✓	10
Standardization/parity not emphasized	✓	●	✓	✓	●	✓	●	✓	✓	×	●	✓	×	×	✓	8
Conflict de-emphasized rather than institutionalized	✓	●	✓	●	●	✓	●	×	●	●	●	✓	×	●	✓	5
Unitarist relations	●	●	×	×	×	●	●	×	●	●	●	✓	×	×	✓	2
Nurturing orientation	●	×	●	●	●	●	●	●	●	●	●	●	●	●	●	0
Strategic aspects																
Customer-orientation to fore	✓	✓	✓	×	●	✓	✓	✓	✓	●	●	✓	✓	✓	✓	11
Integrated initiatives	✓	×	✓	×	●	●	●	●	●	●	●	×	×	×	✓	3
Corporate plan central	✓	●	✓	×	●	●	●	●	●	●	×	×	●	●	✓	3
Speedy decision-making	✓	×	●	×	●	●	●	●	×	×	●	●	×	●	✓	2

Line managers

General/business/line managers to fore	√	√	√	√	√	√	√	√	√	√	√	√	√	√	√	15
Facilitation is prized skill	√	√	√	√	√	√	√	√	√	●	●	●	●	●	√	9
Transformational leadership	√	×	●	●	●	●	√	●	●	●	●	●	●	●	●	4

Key levers

Increased flow of communication	√	√	√	√	√	√	√	√	√	√	√	√	√	√	√	15
Selection is integrated key task	√	√	√	√	√	√	√	√	●	√	√	√	●	√	√	12
Wide-ranging cultural, structural and personnel strategies	√	●	●	√	√	√	√	√	√	√	√	√	●	●	√	12
Teamworking	●	√	√	√	√	√	√	√	●	√	●	√	●	●	√	11
Conflict reduction through culture change	√	√	●	√	√	√	√	√	√	√	√	√	√	√	√	11
Marginalization of stewards	√	●	●	×	√	√	√	●	√	√	√	●	●	√	√	8
Learning companies/heavy emphasis on training	√	●	√	●	●	●	√	●	●	●	√	√	●	●	●	6
Move to individual contracts	●	√	●	●	×	×	●	×	●	√	●	●	×	√	√	3
Performance-related pay, few grades	√	●	×	×	×	×	●	●	●	●	×	×	×	●	●	1
Harmonization	√	●	×	×	×	×	×	×	×	×	×	×	×	●	●	1

Key: √ = yes (existed or were significant moves towards)   × = no   ● = in parts
Source: Storey (1992: 82); Storey and Sisson (1993: 21–2).

"bring" those on the management's side to do their fair share of the work and only one-tenth of our trouble has come from the workman's side' (Taylor, quoted in Bendix, 1956: 280).

Later, however, under the human relations approach, managers were required to encourage and develop workers' creative and emotional needs: 'We must . . . find ways of building up the human organisation within our plants so as to satisfy needs which otherwise result in frustration and irrational demands' (Levinger, quoted in Wilensky and Wilensky, 1951: 280).

In time these ideas, too, were seen as naive or unsound. During the 1970s, the economic, 'instrumental' worker reappeared, and the focus of management activity was again refocused. Now the managers had to assert their authority over the workforce, and had to achieve a close and clear connection between performance and rewards.

Recently a new philosophy of organization – and hence of management – has appeared: human resource strategies. In all conceptions of HRS, the job of the manager is fundamentally reconstructed and is seen as pivotal. A consideration of some influential definitions of HRS will demonstrate the importance attached to management, and the way in which this approach constructs the role (and skills and attitudes) of the manager.

Sisson argues that there are four features associated with HRM:

1 a stress on the integration of personnel policies both with one another and with business planning more generally
2 the locus of responsibility for personnel managers no longer resides with (or is 'relegated to') specialist managers, but is now assumed by senior line management
3 the focus shifts from management–trade union relations to management–employee relations, from collectivism to individualism
4 there is stress on commitment and the exercise of initiative, with managers now donning the role of 'enabler', 'empowerer' and 'facilitator'.

(Sisson, 1990: 5, quoted in Blyton and Turnbull, 1992: 3)

Hendry and Pettigrew (1986) argue that the strategic aspect of HRM consists of four key elements:

1 the use of planning;

2 a coherent approach to the design and management of personnel systems based on an employment policy and manpower strategy, and often underpinned by a 'philosophy';

3 matching HRM activities and policies to some explicit strategy;

4 seeing the people of the organization as a 'strategic resource' for achieving 'competitive advantage'.

It is of course the responsibility of management to define and treat staff as a 'strategic resource'. The authors point to a minimal specification of HRM as a degree of dual integration: coherence of human resource practices with each other, and of all human resource practices with the organization's strategy.

Poole (1990: 3) has defined HRS as follows:

human resource management is viewed as strategic; it involves all managerial personnel . . . it regards people as the most important single asset of the organisation; it is proactive in its relationship with people; and it seeks to enhance company performance, employee 'needs' and societal well being.

If these are the elements of HRS, whose responsibility is it to achieve these goals in practice?

Finally, Guest has argued that the key elements of HRS are:

- Integration of relevant employee activities into general organisational strategies and policies;
- fluid and adaptive organisational structure;
- high quality staff and internal practices to achieve high quality products;
- optimal employee commitment to enterprise goals and practices.

(Guest, 1987, quoted in Cressey and Jones, 1992: 61)

At the level of statements of philosophies of organizational redesign and restructuring, there are various themes that can be seen as common to most definitions of HRS. At its simplest, the overlap has been described by Beaumont (1993: 40) in these terms: 'the key message of the HRM literature is the need to establish a close, two-way relationship between business strategy or planning and

HRM strategy or planning'. The first point in common is the stress on strategic integration: that organizational and personnel structures and systems should be designed to support or 'fit' the strategy of the organization. Second, staff should be managed and treated so that they are committed to the organization and its goals. And third, by achieving strategic integration, there will be real tangible benefits for the organization in terms of critical outputs of quality, performance, etc. Thus managing staff so as to win their commitment (which will rely on a variety of organizational measures and changes) 'is seen as a method of releasing untapped reserves of "human resourcefulness" by increasing employee commitment, participation and involvement' (Blyton and Turnbull, 1992: 4). While the achievement of strategic integration ensures the value of these achievements: 'maximising the economic return from the labour resource by integrating HRM into business strategy' (Blyton and Turnbull, 1992: 4).

However, while there are common elements there are also some crucial differences in approaches to HRS. It is common to distinguish two influential American schools of HRS. These are represented by two key texts from two institutions: Michigan (Fombrun *et al.*, 1984) and Harvard (Beer *et al.*, 1985).

The Michigan group developed the notion of strategic HRM which entailed the interconnection of business strategies, organizational structures and HRM (which meant, in this context, key personnel systems: selection, appraisal, rewards and development). HRM systems were best designed to support the implementation of corporate strategy.

Some key contributors have argued in a classic statement that,

> just as firms will be faced with inefficiencies when they try to implement new strategies with outmoded structures, so they will also face problems of implementation when they attempt to effect new strategies with inappropriate HR systems. The critical management task is to align the formal structure and the HR systems so that they drive the strategic objective of the organisation.
>
> (Fombrum *et al.*, 1984: 37)

At the heart of the Harvard approach (Beer *et al.*, 1984) was the responsibility and capacity of managers to make decisions about the relationship between the organization and its employees such as to maximize the organizational outcomes for key stakeholders. This approach tends to adopt a particular approach to workplace relations: emphasizing unitary, integrative, individualistic systems, undermining workforce organization or collectivist values as outcomes of management choices about the key HRM levers affecting workforce organization relations. This approach focuses on managers' responsibility to manage four key HRM policy areas: employee influence (participation); human resource flow; reward systems; and work systems (work organization). Beer and Spector (1985: 5–6) define this approach as follows:

> A business enterprise has an external strategy: a chosen way of competing in the market place. It also needs an internal strategy: a strategy for how its internal resources are to be developed, deployed, motivated and controlled . . . external and internal strategies must be linked.

But there is another implicit theme common to these definitions of HRS at the level of practical responsibility for ensuring the achievement of HRS. In all models of HRS the role, practice and skills of the manager are, first, redefined, and second, given enormous emphasis. Management itself is reinvented.

This emphasis on management skills is partly a consequence of the fact that frequently these programmes of organizational change – or 'philosophies' of such change, for the evidence on the empirical reality of HRS is at the very least contentious – are associated with precise prescriptions for organizational restructuring. And these restructuring packages have implications for the role of the manager – for example, the move away from centralized, bureaucratic control to devolved, semi-autonomous business units will clearly have implications for the role and responsibilities of managers and for their skills and attitudes. Similarly a move to team work will transform the role of the first-line supervisor, who now becomes a team leader.

HRS is closely associated with particular packages of changes: often those deriving from the 'excellence' literature. Fundamental to the core characteristics of successful companies are a number of a key values: anti-bureaucracy, the breakdown of large

organizational structures into separate strategic business enti-
ties, the devolution of responsibility and authority to lower
organizational levels, the encouragement of 'entrepreneurship',
productivity through people, quality, the dominance of market
principles (even within the organization), and flatter organizational structures. (For example, local authorities are now statu-
torily required to ensure that a number of services previously
supplied by internal departments are now competitively
tendered. The internal supplier is no longer privileged. Within
the Health Service, too, legislation has driven the introduction
of 'market' principles and relationships. Constituent elements of
the total health system must now act as if they were in a market:
they are allocated a budget, they spend this on selected suppliers, etc. Within the private sector, these principles have led
to organizations diversifying non-core activities, and sub-
contracting them, or to establishing customer–supplier relationships *within* the organization.)

HRS writings and the trends they encourage place an enormous value on management and on management skills. It is
these developments which supply the background to the attempt to identify and develop managerial competences. The
appeal and popularity of HRS-type thinking, and the attempt by
many organizations to introduce changes which derive from
HRS thinking, are the background to the recent surge in concern
for the quality of management, in interest in the nature of
management skills, and in attempts to develop management
skills.

During the 1980s the character of management skills became a
focus of national concern in the UK. A number of reports
(Mangham and Silver, 1987; Constable and McCormick, 1987;
Handy, 1987) stressed that Britain's international competitive
position was under severe attack from the forces of globaliz-
ation, and that the country was in danger of losing out to foreign
competition because its stock of managers was not adequately
educated, trained and developed to meet the challenges of
change and global turbulence. In order to guarantee its position
within the world order and promote future growth and economic success it was crucial that 'Britain . . . do more to develop
her managers and do it more systematically' (Handy, 1987: 15).

Thus management is seen as central to organizational effectiveness. 'To a large extent, perhaps even to an increasing extent, it is the competency of managers that will influence the return that an organization will secure from its investment in both human and material capital'(Mangham and Silver, 1987: 2). This conclusion is supported by research data. The Osbaldeston Working Party Report on *The Making of British Managers* (1987), when studying the demand for management training found that the

> most frequently quoted issue [influencing the demand for management development] was an increased recognition of the need to improve managerial performance because of raised expectations and/or pressures in general or because of more specific issues such as increasing UK and international competition, decentralization of organizations, recognition of people management skills.
>
> (Osbaldeston Working Party, 1987: 39)

This report also notes that managers frequently stressed the connection between management development, management skills and business performance.

> Faced with changing markets and increased competition, more and more companies are struggling to re-establish their dominance, regain market share, and in some cases, ensure their survival. Many have come to understand that the key to competitive success is to transform the way they function. They are reducing reliance on managerial authority, formal rules and procedures, and narrow divisions of work. And they are creating teams, sharing information, and delegating responsibility and accountability far down the hierarchy.
>
> (Beer *et al.*, 1990: 158)

When, as a result of environmental pressures, organizations follow the prescriptions of the 'excellence' literature and delayer, devolve and reject organization through rules, formalization and hierarchy in favour of organic, loose structures or networks, management becomes of central importance. Structures are no longer seen as sufficient except in so far as they encourage the development and deployment of managerial skills; hierarchy and organizational systems are not enough if they do not allow the liberation of managers' authority – 'ownership' empowerment. It is under these conditions that managerial skills not only become absolutely critical but also change their nature. Before, management was to a great degree a question of managers' compliance with systems, procedures, regulation and authority, and ensuring the compliance of their subordinates. Management was part of, and sought to achieve, standardization, to reduce difference, individuality and deviation. Now compliance is not enough; achieving obedience is not enough; standardization is no longer virtuous. Now managers are responsible not for obedience but for performance and quality; managers no longer *control*, they *empower*. Thus, Boyatzis (1992: 260) can argue:

> The efficient and effective use of most of an organization's resources depends on the decisions, actions, and thoughts of its managers. The managers are resources that are as vital to organizational performance as its patented products and processes, capital or plant. Understanding the manager as a resource . . . is a prerequisite to organizational improvement efforts whether the focus of these efforts is on strategy, structure, systems, culture or whatever.

So management becomes more important at the same time as it becomes more difficult.

> More and more businesses are doing away with the old bureaucratic incentives and using entrepreneurial opportunity to attract the best talent. Managers must exercise more leadership even as they watch their bureaucratic power slip away. Leadership, in short, is more difficult yet more critical than ever.
>
> (Kanter, 1989a: 91)

Organizational developments (which follow environmental changes) are seen to require new management skills, indeed to require the rewriting of the managerial role altogether. For example, consider the following extract from 'The new managerial work' (Kanter 1989b). This is a classic statement of a commonly held position, specifying various current organizational pressures to which organizations have responded by a

18

series of measures which in turn put pressure on, and make new demands of, management.

Managerial work is undergoing such enormous and rapid change that many managers are reinventing their profession as they go. With little precedent to guide them, they are watching hierarchy fade away and the clear distinctions of title, task, department, even corporation, blur. Faced with extraordinary levels of complexity and interdependency, they watch traditional sources of power erode and the old motivational tools lose their magic.

The cause is obvious. Competitive pressures are forcing corporations to adopt new flexible strategies and structures. Many of these are familiar: acquisitions and divestitures aimed at more focused combinations of business activities, reductions in management staff and levels of hierarchy, increased use of performance-based rewards. Other strategies are less common but have an even more profound effect. In a growing number of companies, for example, horizontal ties between peers are replacing vertical ties as channels of activity and communication. Companies are asking corporate staffs and functional departments to play a more strategic role with greater cross departmental collaboration. Some organizations are turning themselves nearly inside out – buying formerly internal services from outside suppliers, forming strategic alliances and supplier–customer partnerships that bring external relationships inside where they can influence company policy and practice. I call these emerging practices 'post entrepreneurial' because they involve the application of entrepreneurial creativity and flexibility to established businesses. Such changes come highly recommended by the experts who urge organizations to become leaner, less bureaucratic, more entrepreneurial. But so far, theorists have given scant attention to the dramatically altered realities of managerial work in these transformed corporations. We don't even have good words to describe the new relationships. 'Superiors' and 'subordinates' hardly seem accurate, and even 'bosses' and 'their people' imply more control and ownership than managers today actually possess. On top of it all, career paths are no longer straightforward and predictable but have become idiosyncratic and confusing.

Some managers experience the new managerial work as a loss of power because much of their authority used to come from hierarchical position. Now that everything seems negotiable by everyone, they are confused about how to mobilize and motivate staff. For other managers, the shift in roles and tasks offers greater personal power.

(Kanter, 1989b: 80–92)

There is, then, widespread agreement that current environmental developments greatly increase the pressure on organizations to be more effective, more efficient, to do what they do better. Whatever the precise implications for management skills, the overall impression is clear. Few organizations can afford not to change, not to improve performance. The responsibility of managers will be to implement this process of improvement.

However, before considering in more detail what managers should do, and how they should do it, it is first necessary to consider what they actually do.

WHAT DO MANAGERS DO?

─────────────

There are basically two ways of building a model of key aspects of the management role and the skills it requires, so as to develop a view of the basis of managerial effectiveness. One way is to use a descriptive approach which focuses on and builds on what managers actually do, and to build a model of the ideal, or necessary qualities of managers – or the elements of the managerial role, from what managers do, and how they do it. In a sense as we shall see, this is the competence approach.

The other way is to develop a more conceptually inspired view of what management is, based on some view of what managers are for and what their function is. Such a conceptually based view could diverge from actual practice. We shall find that it does so. In fact, the analysis in this book relies largely on the second of these approaches, arguing that what managers *actually* do is not entirely a sensible basis on which to build a model of what they *should* do, unless managers are doing the right things, and doing them right. But how can we decide this?

The discussion of management competences later will encounter this same question – how to establish what managers should do – and will struggle with the same two methods of approach discussed here. However, in this chapter the focus will be on the first method, the study of what managers actually do, the point

21

LIVERPOOL JOHN MOORES UNIVERSITY
LEARNING SERVICES

being to argue that what managers actually do, and how they do it, is not an adequate basis on which to build a model of what they should do, or how they should do it.

What do managers actually do? There is a great deal of information on this which offers important insights. In what follows, which is necessarily selective, some major conclusions will be presented. The sources will be what is called the 'work activity' research – those researchers who studied, by a variety of means, what managers actually do by following them about, getting them to keep diaries, and so on.

Studies of the actual work of managers reveal that their work activities differ markedly from the activities prescribed in management textbooks (Luthans *et al.*, 1985).

In 1982, reporting on work carried out earlier, Mintzberg reported that managers work hard and long. It is a safe bet that events since then (not least organizational changes, environmental challenges and frequent 'downsizing') have increased the amount and the pace of managers' work. It may seem, therefore, unnecessary to ask why managers work so hard and so long. But this is a revealing question, for addressing it throws up some important features of the manager's role, for example, that the manager's job is inherently open-ended: 'there are really no tangible mileposts where he [*sic*] can stop and say, "now my job is finished" . . . the manager is a person with a perpetual preoccupation' (Mintzberg, 1990: 30).

But what about the type of activity that goes on during these long periods of work? The answer suggests a relationship between quantity of work and type of work. Martinko and Gardner (1990: 344) report that 'managerial work is brief, varied, fragmented, spontaneous and highly interpersonal. The managers initiated only about half of their contacts. Almost 40% were initiated by other people and less than 4% were scheduled.' Similarly, Mintzberg found that when he analysed what managers actually did, no activity patterns were evident, except one: that the work occurred in very short episodes – it was highly fragmented, interrupted and brief in duration. The same finding has been noted by others (Carlson, 1951; Stewart, 1967).

Why is managerial work fragmented? Is it a consequence of external pressure, or of managerial choice? Interestingly,

Mintzberg argues that managers themselves determined the duration of their activities. He accounts for this by a process of conditioning, whereby the manager

> is encouraged by the realities of his work to develop a particular personality – to overload himself with work, to do things abruptly, to avoid wasting time, to participate only when the value of participation is tangible, to avoid too great an involvement with one issue. To be superficial is, no doubt, an occupational hazard of managerial work. In order to succeed, the manager must, presumably, become proficient at his superficiality.
>
> (Mintzberg, 1990: 35)

Mintzberg argues that managers could free themselves from interruptions but choose not to do so; that they impose fragmentation on themselves.

Stewart adds that another reason might be that managers need to be available, and that they 'get into the habit of working in a fragmented way and so feel uncomfortable when there are no interruptions'. She also suggests that managers may 'get used to operating by their stream of consciousness so that they switch their attention as soon as they think of something else' (Stewart, 1983: 84).

This discussion of the fragmentation of managerial work, and its origins, is important because it raises for the first time a point which will be considered later in this book: that managers may be encouraged by circumstances, and even by themselves, to behave skilfully in ways which are inefficient, and even, in a sense, incompetent; that is to say, that skill can be counter-productive – or, as Mintzberg, puts it that managers may be proficient at their superficiality.

What else do we know about managers' work? Mintzberg (1990: 35) notes that it is commonly held that managers are systematic, reflective planners, but asserts that the evidence shows that managers like, and gravitate towards, the active aspects of their work – 'activities that are current, specific, and well-defined and that are non-routine'. The managerial environment, and managers' own preferences do not encourage planning, reflection and analysis, but encourage them instead to be 'adaptive information manipulators who prefer the live, concrete situation . . . [and] live action' (p. 38). This point, too, has been noted by other researchers. Stewart (1983: 85) notes that although the traditional picture from management textbooks is of the managers planning, organizing and controlling in a logical, considered and systematic manner, in reality management work consists not of 'ordered and controlled sequences, but of a rapid change of subject matter, requiring the manager to adapt and respond to a wide variety of problems'.

Mintzberg also analyses how far managers control their own work or respond to the requests of others – how far they are reactive and proactive. While acknowledging again that the reality differs from the popular conception in that most managers are unable to control or choose a great many of their activities, he also recognizes that the ability to achieve some control over one's work is probably a significant distinguisher of successful managers.

Mintzberg argues that management work is inherently social. They spend a great deal of time with their subordinates but less time with their superiors. This is interesting because further into the book it will be argued that the management–subordinate relationship is fundamental to management *per se*. So what happens when they spend time with subordinates?

If managers spend much of their time behaving in ways which do not accord with the dictates of the textbooks, they also spend time on activities which are not advocated by these textbooks. Studies of management behaviour have shown that they spend time and effort managing their networks of contacts, seeking to maintain and enlarge their relationships with others (Sayles, 1964). Sayles (1964: 258) remarks that 'The one enduring objective is the effort to build and maintain a predictable, reciprocating system of relationships'. In the same vein, Mintzberg (1980) identifies managers' 'liaison' role, which refers to their focus on, and handling of, relationships, and the ways managers exchange favours and information with others. Kotter (1982: 69) notes that the managers in his study

tried to make others feel legitimately obliged to them by doing favors or by stressing their formal relationships. They acted in ways to encourage others to identify with them. They carefully nurtured their professional reputations in the eyes of others.

Others have noted the political aspects of managers' work, and indeed the focus on networking itself can be seen as a form of interpersonal politicking. A number of writers have noted that managers operate within a politicized system, and that if they are to survive and thrive they need to develop the skills and resources to work politically effectively. Pettigrew (1988) shows how managers' work is assisted or obstructed by their political capacity and position. Within an organization the strength or weakness of an individual or group is related to their structural access to those resources (formal or informal) which ensure compliance with their demands.

Managerial work occurs within a context of differentiated interests, which themselves relate to differences in priorities, viewpoints and resources through vertical and horizontal structural differentiation. Also, Dalton (1959) has shown (what every manager knows) that managers have personal (career) and sectional interests which may conflict with others' goals, or with formal organizational goals, and that managers must pursue them through bargaining, duplicity and bullying.

This analysis of the nature of managerial work is important in a number of ways for our analysis. First, and most importantly, it shows very clearly that it would be highly dangerous to build a model of how managers should behave on the basis of how they behave. The analysis of managers' work shows clearly that it deviates from textbook models:

The manager . . . [is] over-burdened with work. With the increasing complexity of modern organizations and their problems he [*sic*] is destined to become more so. He is driven to brevity, fragmentation and superficiality in his tasks, yet he cannot easily debate them because of the nature of his information. And he can do little to increase his available time or significantly enhance his power to manage. Furthermore, he is driven to focus on that which is current and tangible in his work even though the complex problems facing many organizations call for reflection and a far-sighted perspective.

(Mintzberg, 1980: 173)

Managers may work like this; they may have to work like this, or choose to work like this. But the evidence is that this may not be the best way to work, and therefore these patterns should not form the basis of idealized models of managerial work activity. The patterns of managers' work are regarded by Mintzberg as negative and unhelpful, ill suited to the demands of contemporary managerial work. Many writers have stressed the probable inefficiencies of the brevity and fragmentation of managers' work, stressing in particular the possibility that these features might obstruct reflection and analysis, or might hinder proper attention being given to longer-term, less pressing issues (Stewart, 1989: 2).

Second, these studies raise the question of why managers behave in ways which are apparently inappropriate; one thing that emerges very clearly from Mintzberg's analysis is that these managers are not managing very well. Why do managers put themselves in traps they have constructed themselves?

Stewart suggests interestingly that the fragmented and re-active nature of management work may be a function of managers' preoccupation with interpersonal politicking and networking: She notes that managers give a variety of reasons:

> the expectations of those they work with . . . that they will be available when required to answer queries and to help with problems; the fear that they would not get co-operation unless they were available; the belief that it is their job to be available; and the worry that they would get cut off from what was going on and what they needed to know if people did not think they could go to them freely.

(Stewart, 1983: 83–4)

She also notes the role of habit – and argues that the behaviour of middle and senior managers may be explained in terms of work habits (fragmented work, short attention spans, 'stream of consciousness' type analysis) picked up earlier in their careers as junior managers, which they now apply inappropriately.

Thus for this writer, the reasons for managers' work patterns may lie not in the demands of their managerial role or functions, but in their response to the political realities of their organization, or in the inappropriate persistence of outmoded work habits.

Mintzberg describes what he calls a 'loop' in which managers are caught – a vicious circle – whereby managers respond to environmental demands by working in fragmented, superficial ways. These responses are managers' ways of 'solving' their work-pressure difficulties; but, of course, they make matters worse because they are unsuccessful solutions. Yet this does not stop managers from using them.

This raises a third point: that managers are actually good at and committed to these ways of working. Here, then, is a paradox: a solution which fails and yet is endlessly repeated and which causes or reproduces managers' difficulties and stresses – too much work, time problems, etc. – but which they continue to use; and a set of skilful responses which succeed in producing the outcome the manager wants but which actually do not help resolve the problem and actually reproduce the initial difficulties. How is it that people resolve a difficulty by skilfully and repeatedly producing an outcome which makes matters no better, and possibly makes them worse?

We shall need to look more closely at this situation, and we will do so in later chapters. But at this stage it is necessary to point out that there is a solution to this dilemma, and the solution is broadly along the lines described very briefly and with no elaboration by Mintzberg. The solution requires us to think about what management is, and to identify and develop the skills of managing – of working with and through others effectively. It also requires us to understand why managers may be distracted from this objective. We need to develop a conceptual view of what managers should do based on a view of the management role or function within organizations. This view is not descriptive, indeed it is only necessary to advance the view of management offered here precisely because it is not how managers normally define and execute their managerial work. This allows a comparison of ideal, activities and skills with the reality of how managers actually manage and spend their time.

This point has been made by Hales (1986), who has pointed out that studies of managerial work suffer from lack of a sound theoretical base. Hales suggests that 'what is required is an understanding of how the managerial function is constituted within the overall work process of an organisation', and notes the importance of identifying the focus of the managerial job (Stewart, 1989: 3).

If the way many managers spend much of their time is not merely inappropriate but actually counter-productive, this raises a problem. If a model of management skills and activity cannot be built on managers' actual practice then this must imply that managers may be doing the wrong things, even if they are doing them well and skilfully. How can this be? If managers spend their time in ways which are managerially counter- or unproductive, how do we explain this?

There are three basic possibilities: that managers do not fully know how to manage and so do the best they can from a position of basic ignorance or confusion (the problem of *knowledge*); that they know how to and want to manage well but are unable to (the problem of *capacity* or *skill*); that they know what to do and could do it but choose not to possibly because the way they manage carries benefits (the problem of *choice* or *motivation*). An example of this third possibility would be if managers believed that their career success depended on their political and networking skills and success as much as if not more than on their managerial performance as measured by textbook criteria.

But how could managers, whose very *raison d'être* is (ostensibly) efficiency, purposefully act in ways which are less than fully efficient? How could competent managers choose to act incompetently? This possibility might seem very strange: why should people choose not to do things well? We shall later argue that such a possibility needs to be taken seriously, that managers tend to do what we regard as counter-productive or unproductive things for all three of these reasons. These issues are explored at length in Chapter 8.

4

WHAT ARE THE KEY MANAGEMENT SKILLS?

Recent studies of management education and training (Constable and McCormick, 1987; Handy, 1987, Osbaldeston Working Party, 1987) report a strange paradox. The value of management development and management skills is increasingly accepted, as is evident in the quotations from some of these studies given earlier. Yet there is apparently still very little formal effort to develop management skills. The Osbaldeston Working Party reports on the scarcity of management training – half a day of externally provided courses per manager per year. Mangham and Silver (1987) found that over half the companies in their sample undertook no formal management training at all. So we have a recognition that there is too little management training, a recognition that there needs to be more, and recognition of why it is so important, but hesitation about doing it. Why is this? Mangham and Silver looked at reasons, and found a spread of common-sense views. The most common reasons were expense, inability to spare the managers' time, the preference for on-the-job training, and the view that managers were already sufficiently qualified (Mangham and Silver, 1987: 8).

But these answers do not go far enough: they assume importance only within a situation where managers regard training as unnecessary, irrelevant or likely to be unsuccessful. That is, they will only affect the decision to train or not to train when managers have low expectations of training. These same managers after all, it is reported, value management skills and recognize their strategic value – 'more than half . . . appear to agree that without up-to-date knowledge of management techniques, British management will also be second rate' (Mangham and Silver, 1987: 16).

There is clearly uncertainty and scepticism, however, about what such management training would look like, and it is extraordinary, for example, that the Osbaldeston Working Party says a great deal on the volume of training, on the suppliers of training, and on the methods used, but nothing about what the courses would try to teach.

We have already seen earlier that managers spend a lot of time doing things and behaving in ways which are not productive; however understandable, their time (*qua* managers) is often misspent.

While agreeing with Mintzberg's assessment of how managers spend their time, and how inappropriate this is, given that managerial tasks – particularly those of senior managers – require reflection and a long-term view, we disagree, as will be seen, with his view that the 'brevity, fragmentation and superficiality' of managers' activities are forced upon them and, by implication, cannot be avoided. These aspects of managers' work are the result of powerful forces which we will address later, but they *can* be avoided, as we shall also consider later.

There are two implications of the way managers spend their time. First, if managers spend a lot of time doing inappropriate things, then it may be problematic to model how managers should behave on the basis of how they do behave – a conception of desired managerial behaviour may also need reference to a theoretically driven model. We shall offer one.

Second, if managers spend a lot of their time behaving in inappropriate ways, we must ask why this is, not least because if we are to convert them to preferred behaviours we have to understand the grounds for their current actions. We shall return to this in due course, for we shall argue that this is no accident; it is a systematic product of various structures, values and forces which understandably constrain and encourage managers to behave in a less than fully competent manner. These forces need to be described and understood if they are to be overcome.

The new managerial skills competences

What, then, are the key attributes or competences that managers need in order to face and survive the challenges they and their organizations face?

Many influential management writers have attempted to identify the key management skills of the new organization. Morgan, for example, like many other writers, argues that in fundamental ways the 'new' organization responds to environmental developments and challenges:

> The pace and complexity of change are as likely to increase as to decrease in the years ahead. Few, if any, organisations can be sure of a secure future, as scientific and technological developments can transform the very ground on which they have learned to operate. Change can come from 'out of the blue'. Traditional competences or market niches can be challenged by new technologies, generating new skills and new products.
>
> (Morgan, 1988: 2)

He then lists nine areas of competency (Figure 4.1). All these competences are clearly and closely related to identifying and responding to key environmental challenges, and to managing competently within the 'new' appropriate form of organization.

However, the problem with Morgan's list is that no matter how intuitively attractive it might be, it is at best a summary of the author's views, or his view of some managers' views. Its status as a research-based finding is possibly questionable; furthermore, even if its pedigree is impeccable, how useful is it? How secure are these generalizations? Indeed, how operational are these recommendations? The problem with all attempts to identify the

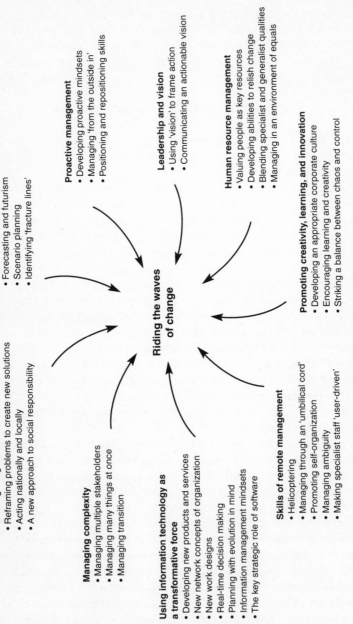

Figure 4.1 Morgan's list of management competences
Source: Morgan (1988: 3)

Developing contextual competences
• Building bridges and alliances
• Reframing problems to create new solutions
• Acting nationally and locally
• A new approach to social responsibility

Managing complexity
• Managing multiple stakeholders
• Managing many things at once
• Managing transition

Using information technology as a transformative force
• Developing new products and services
• New network concepts of organization
• New work designs
• Real-time decision making
• Planning with evolution in mind
• Information management mindsets
• The key strategic role of software

Skills of remote management
• Helicoptering
• Managing through an 'umbilical cord'
• Promoting self-organization
• Managing ambiguity
• Making specialist staff 'user-driven'

Reading the environment
• Scanning and intelligence functions
• Forecasting and futurism
• Scenario planning
• Identifying 'fracture lines'

Proactive management
• Developing proactive mindsets
• Managing 'from the outside in'
• Positioning and repositioning skills

Leadership and vision
• Using 'vision' to frame action
• Communicating an actionable vision

Human resource management
• Valuing people as key resources
• Developing abilities to relish change
• Blending specialist and generalist qualities
• Managing in an environment of equals

Promoting creativity, learning, and innovation
• Developing an appropriate corporate culture
• Encouraging learning and creativity
• Striking a balance between chaos and control

Riding the waves of change

managerial skills for the new organization is that the status and practical value of the recommendation are often very shaky. However attractive the suggestion, these problems remain, and it is precisely for this reason that the competence movement has recently gathered momentum, because of its claim to offer a way out of these problems.

The competence approach

Recent attempts to identify key managerial skills have centred on the notion of managerial competence, and it is to this important and influential approach to managerial skills and behaviour that we now turn. First, we discuss the competence approach, and describe briefly the key managerial competences that have been identified in two major statements on the subject. Then we assess the approach and consider some problem areas.

There is nothing new in seeking to identify the qualities an effective manager needs. The management literature is full of such analyses. But, however appealing these analyses may be, they are, in the majority of cases, ultimately subjective and impressionistic. It is thus hard to pick from among them, except by exercising even more subjectivity. We can all devise lists of key management skills (or competences); but how are we to judge between them? What is new about the competence movement is the way this concern to identify the core behaviours of managers has been pursued – that is, the approach and methodology. For the important thing about the competence approach is not just the product of the approach, but the approach itself.

First, however, what is a competence? As Woodruffe has noted, the term is somewhat slippery. He remarks: 'It often seems to be used as an umbrella term to cover almost anything that might directly or indirectly affect job performance' (Woodruffe, 1992: 16). However, while there are conflicting accounts of what the term means, Woodruffe and other commentators agree that the term is concerned with the 'behaviours' people need to display in order to perform effectively.

Clearly competences and skills inhabit the same ground, but the two are not the same. The term 'skills' refers to the qualities and abilities of the individual. Competences, on the other hand, focus not on the individual, but on the activity. All competence systems are, therefore, based upon explicit behavioural or outcome-based statements. In other words, they focus on actual performance – on what people *can do* rather than what they *know*.

An important aspect of competence is that they are research-based, and are derived from the study of practising managers. Specific competences are identified through research which involves the people who are actually involved in specific work roles. According to Woodruffe (1992:17), for example,

> a competency is a dimension of overt, manifest behaviour that allows a person to perform competently. Behind it must be both the ability and desire to behave in that competent way. For example, the person competent at selling will need a competency that includes listening. In turn that includes knowing how to listen and choosing to listen. Put more generally, people will only produce competent action in a situation if they know how to and if they value the consequences of the expected outcomes of the action.

Thus, competences are represented as distinguishable from aspects of the job. Rather they deal with the capacities, dispositions and attributes – universally described as 'behaviours' – that people need to display in order to do a job effectively and not with the job itself. In other words, 'competence' refers to certain characteristics that a person exhibits which results in effective job performance (Klemp, 1980; Woodruffe, 1992). These characteristics are regarded as generic, though they do receive different emphasis depending, for example, on management level or on the sector within which the organization in question is located (Boyatzis, 1982).

The competence approach has been distinguished from 'traditional' approaches to the assessment of key work qualities by Fletcher (1992), who distinguishes 'traditional' and competence approaches on a number of dimensions, as shown in Table 4.1.

Table 4.1 Traditional and competence approaches contrasted

	Traditional	*Competence-based*
Concept	Assessment of learning ability or achievement	Assessment of actual performance in a work role
Foundation	Curricula, defined centrally by teaching staff/divisional boards	Explicit standards of required performance defined by industry (UK) or by research using 'excellent' performers (USA)
Assessment requirements	Assessment is an integral part of learning programmes	Assessment is independent of any learning programme
Evidence	Assessment evidence drawn from course assignments/exams	Assessment evidence collected from actual workplace performance supplemented by other methods
	Types of evidence predetermined by course syllabus	Types of evidence governed only by rules for quality of evidence
	Assessment is norm-referenced	Assessment is criterion-referenced (UK), criterion-validated (USA), and individualized

Source: Fletcher (1992: 21)

The aim of the competence approach is to provide an integrated system whereby those generic characteristics that distinguish competent managerial performance are identified, existing and required levels of competence are assessed, and any resultant gaps are addressed through performance review and management training and development.

Boyatzis (1982: 21) develops this definition with particular reference to the generic quality of competences:

Because job competencies are *underlying characteristics*, they can be said to be generic. A generic characteristic may be apparent in many forms of behaviour, or a wide variety of different actions. Baldwin (1958) explained that when a person performs an act (i.e., demonstrates a specific behaviour) which has a result or several results (i.e., outcomes), it is also expression of a characteristic or of several characteristics. Actions, their results, and the characteristics being expressed do not necessarily have a one-to-one correspondence. . . . The action, or specific behaviour, is the manifestation of a competency in the context of the demands and requirements of a specific job and particular organizational environment. Given a different job or different organizational environment, the competency may be evident through other specific actions. In the same manner, the result of the action (i.e., the effect it has) is related to the requirements and setting in which it occurs.

The point Boyatzis makes here is about the difficulty of making inferences about innate qualities from samples of behaviour: how *representative* is a particular sample of behaviour? How *revealing* is the behaviour? Clearly this issue goes to the heart of an attempt to identify key management skills, attributes or 'competences' that is based and builds on measured qualities. A descriptively based approach is dependent on the representativeness of the data. We shall argue that, however representative the data on which competences are based, there is an inherent difficulty in trying to identify what people *should* do on the basis of what they *do* do.

Thus the competence approach claims to establish a crucial link between personal qualities and behaviours which enhance or achieve organizational effectiveness. No wonder so many organizations are using it.

A key feature of the competence approach is that it focuses not simply on qualities or inputs (for example, the knowledge included in training course content, or educational or professional qualifications, or 'intelligence') but on outputs – behaviours which research suggests characterize the successful manager. So rather than saying that a successful manager needs to have studied certain courses, or to have so many years of certain sorts of defined experience (all of which have been regarded as means of gaining key knowledge and skills), the competence approach, on a research basis, argues that effective managers need the wherewithal to be able to do certain sorts of things which have been systematically identified by research as critical to role success. The competence approach broadly tries to identify job-relevant behaviours which are held to have an impact on performance, rather than individual qualities.

There are currently two major approaches to competences: the 'personal characteristics' approach of Boyatzis which seeks to identify the distinctive, personal characteristics of competent managers; and that of the UK Management Charter Initiative (MCI) which adopts a functional approach to competence – seeking to identify concretely the work functions which a competent manager should be capable of performing. There are differences between the US and UK approach to competences. The key distinction, noted by Woodruffe (1992: 17), is 'between aspects of the job at which the person is competent, [UK] and aspects of the person that enable him or her to be competent [USA].'

The American approach to competence also emphasizes the distinction between *threshold* competences which all job holders require – the competences necessary for someone to fill the job – and *differentiator* competences which distinguish the outstanding manager from the average manager.

The British approach uses a different methodology which reflects its greater focus on the task – the methodology uses a task-oriented technique, 'functional analysis',

> to identify the necessary roles, tasks and duties of the occupation rather than the skills of successful role incumbents. This yields an extensive list of elements of competence grouped under major functional or key role areas, with performance criteria developed to indicate minimum competence levels.
>
> (Iles, 1992: 117)

The American approach, because it is more people-focused, is concerned to identify the characteristics which distinguish successful role incumbents.

Nevertheless, despite differences in methodology and application, the two approaches generate similar findings and share similar limitations and strengths. Both use a distinctive methodology which seeks to identify and measures management competence on the basis of thorough-going research. However, the issues addressed by the research associated with each approach differ. The methodology used in the competence approach is important because it is at the same time a great strength of the approach, and, some have argued, one of its limitations.

Table 4.2 summarizes the main elements and stages of the methodology for studying competences in the 'personal characteristics' tradition. The methodology uses and relies on the ideas and experiences of managers. It begins with an analysis of measures of job performance and how performance can be assessed. Next, job element analysis produces a list of weighted characteristics that managers perceive as important in distinguishing superior from average performers. This analysis is conducted by an expert panel of senior managers. The third step – behavioural event interviewing – involves individual interviews with current incumbents of the job. These interviews test the conclusions of the expert panel and aim to produce a detailed empirical description of the competences which job holders must have. It thus tests the conclusions of the expert panel. The fourth and fifth steps identify or devise tests and measures of the competences identified by behavioural event interviewing. These tests are then related back to job performance criteria – so that there is now a link between job performance and job competence through tests and measures. The loop is closed (Boyatzis, 1982: 41).

Boyatzis's competences model is based on a sample of over 2000 managers who were used to determine the competences common to those who were identified as effective. Boyatzis identifies thirteen competences, which are listed in the centre column of Table 4.3. As can be seen, Boyatzis identifies six 'clusters' of competences. Boyatzis relates these competences to

Table 4.2   The job competence assessment method

Steps	Activities	Results
Identification of criterion measure	Choose an appropriate measure of job performance. Collect data on managers.	Job performance data on managers.
Job element analysis	Generate list of characteristics perceived to lead to effective and/or superior job performance. Obtain item rating by managers. Compute weighted list of characteristics. Analyse clusters of characteristics.	A weighted list of characteristics perceived by managers to relate to superior performance. A list of the clusters into which these characteristics can be grouped.
Behavioural event interviews	Conduct behavioural event interviews. Code interviews for characteristics or develop the code and then code the interviews. Relate the coding to job performance data.	A list of characteristics hypothesized to distinguish effective and/or superior from poor or less effective job performance. A list of validated characteristics, or competences.
Tests and measures	Choose tests and measures to assess competences identified in prior two steps as relevant to job performance. Administer tests and measures and score them. Relate scores to job performance data.	A list of validated characteristics, or competences, as assessed by these tests and measures.
Competency model	Integrate results from prior three steps. Statistically and theoretically determine and document causal relationships among the competences and between the competences and job performance.	A validated competency model.

Source: Boyatzis (1982)

Table 4.3 Summary of Boyatzis's competence analysis

Cluster	Competency	Threshold competency
Goal and action management cluster	Concern with impact (skill, motive). Diagnostic use of concepts (skill, social role). Efficiency orientation (skill, motive, social role). Proactivity (skill, social role).	Logical thought (skill, social role).
Leadership cluster	Conceptualization (skill). Self-confidence (skill, social role). Use of oral presentations (skill, social role).	Logical thought (skill, social role).
Human resource management cluster	Managing group process (skill). Use of socialized power (skill, social role).	Accurate self-assessment (skill). Positive regard (skill).
Directing subordinates cluster	Developing others (skill, social role).	Spontaneity (skill). Use of unilateral power (skill, social role).
Focus on others cluster	Perceptual objectivity (skill). Self-control (trait). Stamina and adaptability (trait).	
Specialized knowledge		Specialized knowledge (social role).

Source: Boyatzis (1982)

key aspects of managerial activity and the management role. Having identified the competences, he explores their connections with aspects of the management role or management functions (of which he distinguishes five: the planning function; the organizing function; the controlling function, the motivating function; and the co-ordinating function). He establishes the connection between competence and management function through the identification of a number of 'tasks' associated with the function, and requiring the competences (Table 4.4).

A final element added by Boyatzis to his analysis is the connection between aspects of what he calls the 'organizational environment' – key organizational systems and processes, which relate to organizational departments, disciplines and functions – and competence clusters.

By drawing these connections, Boyatzis argues the particular importance of different competence clusters for different functions. An issue that immediately arises here is: although it may well be the case that managers are required to do many (some, all) things, should they all be seen as fundamental elements of management *per se*, or are some of them simply things that managers are often required to do as well as managing? This question (and Boyatzis's list of competences) thus lead us to a consideration of the key elements of the managerial role, and this will be considered briefly in the next section.

The MCI approach identifies four key managerial roles which relate to nine *units* of competence (see Table 4.5). These competences are then related to key work activities and behaviours – things that managers with each competence would be able to do: these are the *elements* of competence.

As well as the units of competence, MCI also identifies personal competences (Figure 4.2). These relate 'to the way in which you carry out your job, and could point to valuable improvements you could make' (MCI, 1991: 6).

Because personal competence is an intrinsic part of any competent manager's job, the M.C.I. has developed a personal competence framework. This framework serves to identify the underlying personal qualities, skills and

Table 4.4 The relationship between management functions and competence clusters

Function	Tasks	Relevant competency clusters
Planning	1 Determining the goals of the organization.	Competences in the goal and action management cluster.
	2 Establishing plans of action for achieving those goals.	
	3 Determining how the plan should be accomplished.	
	4 Communicating this to others.	Competences in the leadership cluster.
Organizing	1 Determining what people and resources are needed to accomplish the plan.	Competences in the goal and action management cluster.
	2 Determining how these people and resources should be structured to do it.	Competences in the leadership cluster.
	3 Establishing the standards of performance.	
	4 Communicating this to others.	Competences in the human resource management cluster.
Controlling	1 Monitoring performance of individuals and groups.	Competences in the goal and action management cluster.
	2 Providing feedback to individuals and groups.	Competences in the directing subordinates cluster and human resource management cluster.
	3 Rewarding or disciplining based on performance.	
Motivating	1 Building commitment, identity, pride, and spirit in the organization.	Competences in the human resource management cluster and the leadership cluster.
	2 Stimulating an interest in work.	
	3 Developing capability in subordinates.	Competences in the directing subordinates cluster.
Co-ordinating	1 Stimulating co-operation among departmental, divisions, and other work groups.	Competences in the human resource management cluster and the focus on other clusters.
	2 Negotiating resolution of conflicts and differences.	
	3 Representing the organization to outside groups.	Competences in the leadership cluster.

Source: Boyatzis (1982)

Table 4.5   MCI key roles, units of competence and their associated elements of competence

	Units	Elements
Manage operations	1.1 Maintain and improve service and product operations.	1.1 Maintain operations to meet quality standards. 1.2 Create and maintain the necessary conditions for productive work.
	1.2 Contribute to the implementation of change in services, products and systems.	2.1 Contribute to the evaluation of proposed changes to services, products and systems. 2.2 Implement and evaluate changes to services, products and systems.
Manage finance	1.3 Recommend, monitor and control the use of resources.	3.1 Make recommendations for expenditure. 3.2 Monitor and control the use of resources.
Manage people	1.4 Contribute to the recruitment and selection of personnel.	4.1 Define future personnel requirements. 4.2 Contribute to the assessment and selection of candidates against team and organizational requirements.
	1.5 Develop teams, individuals and self to enhance performance.	5.1 Develop and improve teams through planning and activities. 5.2 Identify, review and improve development activities for individuals. 5.3 Develop oneself within the job.
	1.6 Plan, allocate and evaluate work carried out by teams, individuals and staff.	6.1 Set up and update work objectives for teams and individuals. 6.2 Plan activities and determine work methods to achieve objectives. 6.3 Allocate work and evaluate teams, individuals and self against objectives. 6.4 Provide feedback to teams and individuals on their performance.
	1.7 Create, maintain and enhance effective working relationships.	7.1 Establish and maintain the trust and support of one's subordinates. 7.2 Establish and maintain the trust and support of one's immediate manager. 7.3 Establish and maintain relationships with colleagues. 7.4 Identify and minimize interpersonal conflict. 7.5 Implement disciplinary and grievance procedures. 7.6 Counsel staff.
Manage information	1.8 Seek, evaluate and organize information for action.	8.1 Obtain and evaluate information to aid decision making 8.2 Record and store information.
	1.9 Exchange information to solve problems and make decisions.	9.1 Lead meetings and group discussions to solve problems and make decisions. 9.2 Contribute to discussions to solve problems and make decisions. 9.3 Advise and inform others.

Source: MCI (1991)

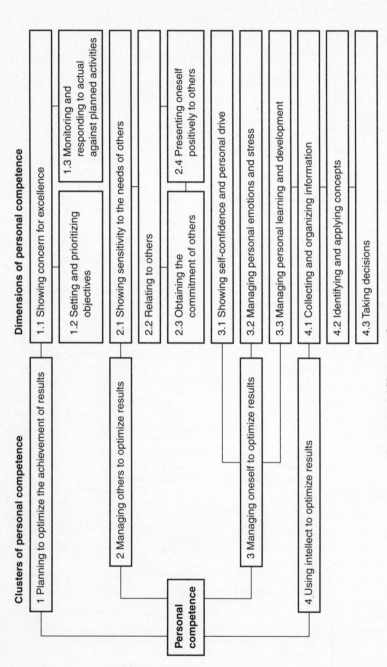

Clusters of personal competence

1 Planning to optimize the achievement of results

2 Managing others to optimize results

3 Managing oneself to optimize results

4 Using intellect to optimize results

Personal competence

Dimensions of personal competence

1.1 Showing concern for excellence

1.2 Setting and prioritizing objectives

1.3 Monitoring and responding to actual against planned activities

2.1 Showing sensitivity to the needs of others

2.2 Relating to others

2.3 Obtaining the commitment of others

2.4 Presenting oneself positively to others

3.1 Showing self-confidence and personal drive

3.2 Managing personal emotions and stress

3.3 Managing personal learning and development

4.1 Collecting and organizing information

4.2 Identifying and applying concepts

4.3 Taking decisions

Figure 4.2 MCI personal competences

attributes which are associated with effective management behaviour. The significance of these personal characteristics is often more a matter of degree than of absolute presence or absence. However, as developing managers, it is important that all managers be aware of their own personal competence in order to continue to improve and respond to changing needs within their work environment.

(MCI, 1991: 90)

We shall return to these in some detail later in this book, for these personal competences and their associated dimensions are pertinent to the skills identified as necessary for achieving personal effectiveness through what is called here the management of performance.

Within the competence movement, as well as the distinction between USA and UK, there is a useful distinction between generic and specific competences. *Specific* competences are those that are claimed to be relevant to successful management within particular organizations. There have been a number of studies aimed at identifying specific competences within the UK. A number of major companies (Cadbury Schweppes, W.H. Smith, BP, Manchester Airport, National Westminster, National and Provincial, Rank Xerox) have attempted to identify the middle management competences. (For a useful summary of the findings of many of these studies, see Woodruffe, 1992: 23.) *Generic* competences, on the other hand, arise from the suggestion that there may be some common competences for middle and senior management posts. Thornton and Byham (1982), for example, have offered a list of the universal competences of top management (see Table 4.6).

The competence approach has not been immune to criticism, some of which is germane to our concern to identify the key skills of management. The limitations identified are pertinent to the approach advocated in these chapters, which offers a way forward, incorporating the best of the approach but focusing it on some specific core features of the management role.

One major criticism of the approach takes a variety of forms. This argues that the methodology employed, although thorough

Table 4.6 Universal competences of top management

Oral presentation	Negotiation
Oral communication	Analysis
Written communication	Judgement
Organizational sensitivity	Creativity
Organizational awareness	Risk taking
Extra-organizational sensitivity	Decisiveness
Extra-organizational awareness	Technical and
Planning and organizing	professional knowledge
Delegation	Energy
Management control	Range of interests
Development of subordinates	Initiative
Sensitivity	Tolerance of stress
Individual leadership	Adaptability
Group leadership	Independence
Tenacity	Motivation

Source: Thornton and Byham (1982)

and well-executed, focuses on just some activities and skills and not others, that it therefore focuses on a limited range of competences and pays less attention to future job requirements (which must be derived from some theoretical view of these needs), that it focuses on the easily measurable, and that because it is entirely descriptive it is unable to organize and prioritize the empirical findings for that requires a concept of the key managerial functions and activities, and that cannot be derived from description.

One version of the criticism is to note the essentially static, present-focused aspect of the competence approach. If organizations are changing, and changing rapidly in ways which have implications for the management role (and this book has certainly argued this position), then will a competence model based on descriptions and analyses of what current managers do and have done, be sufficient? Is there a risk that such an approach will describe yesterday's requirements and not tomorrow's?

Boyatzis himself is well aware of this criticism, but obviously feels that to incorporate its implications would seriously undermine his methodology. It is worth quoting his defence against what he correctly identifies as a major challenge to the value of his findings in a rapidly changing world, because it very clearly articulates the two sides of the issue: the methodological virtue, as Boyatzis sees it, of an empirically driven descriptive approach, against a more prescriptive, subjective position. His view is clear:

> The use of any performance measure may suffer from a criticism concerning the use of a 'current' measure of performance. A measure of performance that is currently in use by an organization or by the people in it only reflects effective performance as they see it. The use of such a measure does not confront the problem of potential short-sightedness of the entire organization, or of its possible lack of understanding of some larger significance that a different basis for determining effectiveness or a different set of goals may have. Of course, the problem with any other measure of performance of effectiveness is that it emerges from an individual's or group's ideal image of an appropriate goal for the organization or the people in specific jobs within that organization. Such a measure, which may be theoretically or philosophically sound, is a relative subjective judgement. Therefore it is based on a particular theory or set of values. To avoid embroilment in a philosophical argument it can be said that the performance measures used in this study seemed to be the best available. Instead of imposing some arbitrary, theoretical or value-based assumption as to what constitutes effectiveness as a manager each organization involved in these studies determined what effectiveness was, or who was demonstrating it, in the context of its goals and objectives.
>
> (Boyatzis, 1982: 434)

This passage is most revealing. First, it starkly sets out the two positions; and Boyatzis's preference is displayed not only by the argument but also by the language he uses. Clearly the suggestion that an analysis of management skills or competence could be driven by forces other than a descriptive-based methodology which builds analysis on current practice, is regarded as deeply threatening. And yet surely, as is argued elsewhere in this chapter, there is a need for a conceptually based view of the management role and of core management skills if only to assist selection from or prioritizing of the competences described in the models. We need to separate the competences of managing from the competences required by a selection of managers who do an awful lot more in their work than just manage others.

There is, therefore, a risk with competence methodology that its very technical strength is also its weakness – that it is descriptive, present-focused, and constitutes a closed self-fulfilling loop. Cockerill (1989: 52), for example, remarks:

> Many validation studies display a sterile, closed loop of research. Techniques such as repertory grid are used to elicit 'effective' dimensions of behaviours from the minds of managers; managers, often the same ones, assess participants against these dimensions at an assessment centre: managers are then asked to validate the assessment centre by using the same or similar dimensions of behaviour to rate the 'job performance' of participants. This method tells us more about the reliability with which managers can rate the same dimensions of behaviour in different settings than it does about the relationship between these dimensions and organizational performance. Additionally, this approach can formalize the self-perpetuation of a cadre of managers who, consciously or not, are using the process to select in their own image when circumstances have changed when they have no evidence to demonstrate that this image is significantly related to organizational performance.

It has also been argued that the competence methodology, because it sensibly seeks to place the analysis of management competence on an empirical basis of measurement, may have given insufficient attention to those key management skills which are hard to measure, but none the less crucial, such as the 'soft' personal qualities – assertiveness, impact, creativity, sensitivity and intuition – which are difficult to measure under any circumstances (Jacobs, 1989).

If, as noted, the competence methodology is present-focused

and excessively descriptive, it may not help us identify the competences for changing (or changed) conditions. As the role of managers changes so do the skills that managers need to use in order to be successful. And the competence models may focus heavily on competences that are most appropriate for stable, bureaucratic environments.

Nevertheless, some work has been done to identify the competences for change. Schroder (1989), for example identifies 11 high-performance managerial competences (see Table 4.7). This list – and other inventories of competences for the future – is not derived from the classic competence methodology described earlier. At best, if these competences for change are research-based, they are the result of the statistical amalgamation of the thoughts and intuitions of practising managers. As such they are clearly of interest. But while they are derived from the conceptual models (of the qualities of the manager of the future, or of the organization of the future, etc.) of the managers whose opinions were gathered (and are, therefore, clearly are as good and robust as the models on which they are based) these models or concepts of management remain implicit, undisclosed resources on which the lists of competences are based.

Limitations to competence

There are a number of difficulties or limitations inherent in the competence approach: that the competence literature is inherently focused on the measurable; that it deals with existing values and attitudes of those who produce the data, that it is past-focused; and that it moves illegitimately from the descriptive to the prescriptive.

The more severe limitation of the competence literature is inherent in its approach. The analysis of competences is derived from managers' assessments and views. But the value of these views may be limited. Also, considerable confusion exists as to the nature of competences: 'are they general personality traits, general ability traits, transferable skills, knowledge and

Table 4.7 High performance management competences

Information search
Gathers many different kinds of information and uses a wide variety of sources to build a rich informational environment in preparation for decision-making in the organization.

Concept formation
Builds frameworks or models or forms concepts, hypotheses or ideas on the basis of information; becomes aware of patterns, trends and cause/effect relations by linking disparate information.

Conceptual flexibility
Identifies feasible alternatives or multiple options in planning and decision-making; holds different options in focus simultaneously and evaluates their pros and cons.

Interpersonal search
Uses open and probing questions, summaries, paraphrasing etc. to understand the ideas, concepts and feelings of another; can comprehend events, issues, problems, opportunities from the viewpoint of another person.

Managing interaction
Involves others and is able to build co-operative teams in which group members feel valued and empowered and have shared goals.

Developmental orientation
Creates a positive climate in which individuals increase the accuracy of their awareness of their own strengths and limitations and provides coaching, training and developmental resources to improve performance.

Impact
Uses a variety of methods (e.g. persuasive arguments, modelling behaviour, inventing symbols, forming alliances and appealing to the interest of others) to gain support for ideas, strategies and values.

Self-confidence
States own 'stand' or position on issues; unhesitatingly takes decisions when required and commits self and others accordingly; expresses confidence in the future success of the actions to be taken.

Presentation
Presents ideas clearly, with ease and interest so that the other person (or audience) understand what is being communicated; uses technical, symbolic, non-verbal and visual aids effectively.

Proactive orientation
Structures the task for the team; implements plans and ideas; takes responsibility for all aspects of the situation.

Achievement orientation
Possesses high internal work standards and sets ambitious yet attainable goals; wants to do things better, to improve, to be more effective and efficient; measures progress against targets.

Source: Cockerill (1989), Personnel Management, Sept.

behaviour, or organisation-specific skills, knowledge and be-haviour? The truth is that they draw upon all these psychological attributes' (Sparrow and Bogdano, 1993:52). There are also questions about the value of a competence approach such as that of the MCI, which focuses essentially on aspects of the job.

But another and potentially more damaging criticism of the competence approach is that it is lacking in any conceptually based understanding of the manager's role; its only reference to concepts is to the concepts or models which inform manager's thinking, but which are left uninterrogated and unidentified by the competence methodology. The competence approach runs the risk of enshrining the concepts of the research respondents in definitions of the manager's role but without ever confronting and challenging these concepts. Managers use implicit, often unacknowledged, un-noticed and un-discussable models, as-sumptions and recipes. These guide their actions and their assessments of the necessary and virtuous qualities of organiz-ational heroes. Despite the power and prevalence of these managers' models, we cannot use them as a basis for the identification of key managerial competences.

Instead, this approach focuses on what managers think about other managers' management performance. Mangham and Silver (1987:31), for example report that when asked about management skills,

> many of the respondents provide replies in terms of func-tional skills at a level of abstraction that is of little value, and . . . their vocabulary of skills is limited. Many, particularly those doing little or no training of their managers, were unable or unwilling to specify the qualities, attributes and skills required of, for example, junior managers.

The researchers attribute the managers' difficulties in terms of *conceptual poverty* – concepts, they note, are essential for organiz-ing information and establishing connections and patterns in it. This is precisely what we shall attempt here. Our model of core management skills is based not on descriptions of what managers do, nor on extrapolations of managers' conceptions of good and bad managers (although we shall acknowledge and use such material) but on a model of what management is, of what the role involves.

Thus we need a more conceptual and theoretical understanding of what management is and what managers need to be able to do, an understanding which goes beyond the mere mapping, however thorough, of what current managers think constitutes good and bad managers. What follows constitutes such a change of approach: we shall build a conception of management based on a view of the responsibilities and tasks of the management role or position in the modern organization. We shall then identify the key tasks of management the key skills required to achieve these tasks.

The discussion of competences has been somewhat theoretical so far. Some of the strengths and weaknesses of the competence approach have been identified. We must now ground this discussion through the identification of some practical conclusions.

First, it is true that any analysis of what managers need to be good at in order to manage well must be based on an analysis of what managers do when they manage (which might be rather different from what they do in their work). In other words, it is necessary to separate the essentially managerial aspects (and skills) of a person's job from the many other things that a manager might be asked to do which are not in themselves inherently managerial. Models of management skills must be based on analyses of managerial work, and what it requires. So far, then, the competence approach is valuable in that it attempts to do precisely this. However, its approach is flawed.

Second, if we are to make progress with the discussion, identification and development of key managerial competences we must consider not only what managers actually do but also crucially what they *should* do. *Description* must be carefully differentiated from *prescription*, for it is neither possible nor useful to build prescription on the basis of description. Managers may not – indeed we know, from earlier discussions, do not – do what they should do.

One important reason for this is that one of the features of any organization is that it offers a cultural view of one's own and others' roles, and how these should be performed. Thus organizational cultures are likely to colour managers' conceptions of effective and ineffective management behaviour. When asked to describe an effective manager, managers will not simply refer to some neutral body of observation, but will call on their 'stock of recipes' – the formulae that explain what is happening and advise what ought to happen. Such recipes describe, among other things the processes necessary to achieve certain sorts of organizational results – to get on, to manage workers, to please a client. As such they would significantly affect notions of successful management behaviour.

Consider a hypothetical organization. Here 'managers' were part of, and highly committed to, an organizational culture and history in which they were a social and intellectual elite with a right to manage staff who were intellectually, morally and socially inferior. Within this organization the structure was highly hierarchical and elitist, with enormous differences in privilege and conditions between two differentiated strata of managers and workers. Within this organization arrogance, elitism, deference and subordination were rife. Communications were one-way; harsh discipline was enforced; consultation unheard of. Management consisted in giving orders and enforcing discipline. Staff were constantly under surveillance and supervision. Now imagine that these managers were asked to consider and to identify examples of effective management. They would almost certainly give answers which were highly influenced by the models in their heads and by their observations of practices they witnessed around them which articulated these models. These answers would tell us much about the managers' mental and ideological constructs. They would tell us much even about prevalent practices within the organization. But would they tell us anything about 'good' management? Now if your answer to this highly loaded question is negative, then we must ask what conception of good management you used when you came to this conclusion. For you have just been doing what the competence approach cannot do: you have been using a conceptual model of what managers should do in order to assess the value of what they do do. Our conviction in this book is that the identification of the necessary qualities and competences of managers must, ultimately, be based on such a premise.

Third, we need to identify what managers need to be able to do (or must know and understand) in order to achieve the key management competences. It is one thing, for example, to say that a key management competence is 'managing others to optimize results', and even to add that this will require 'showing sensitivity to the needs of others, relating to others, obtaining the commitment of others', and so on. But how can these be achieved? What are the potential barriers to success? Too often the competence approach to this question is to break down the competence into smaller and smaller units. But these units, even the micro-units, still describe what needs to be done, they do not describe what the manager has to do, or avoid, in order to do it.

Fourth, and crucially, we need to be able to prioritize these competences, to decide how they work together, which are critical, which are subsidiaries of others, and so on. Lists of competences are just that – lists. We have suggested that many of the items on the lists are indeed important. But how do we know that they are important and how can we decide which are more or less important than others? Again, the answer to this can only come from some conceptually informed view of what managers must be able to do to manage well. If we are to offer a view of the things that managers must be able to do (as we do here) we must be able to justify this view – to show why these activities, skills or competences are critical.

In the next chapter we start with the first of these issues: what managers need to be able to do in order to manage well.

5

THE MANAGEMENT ROLE

Management may be regarded from different perspectives and defined in terms of very different elements – for example, Fayol lists forecasting and planning, organize, command, co-ordination and control; Wilfred Brown emphasizes managerial authority and hierarchy; Gulick lists planning, organizing, staffing, directing, co-ordinating, reporting, budgeting; to say nothing of Mintzberg's list of managerial roles, discussed earlier. How can we steer a path through all these?

One way forward is to stop worrying about what may look like definitional confusion and chaos, and try to see these confusions as themselves possibly representing aspects of a complex and highly differentiated organizational role. Beyond this, it will help if we identify aspects of this multi-faceted role, and also identify those aspects which will not be considered here, however important they may be.

Critical to this clarification and focusing are two distinctions: first between the role and the position, and secondly between aspects of the role. These could be seen as a pair of axes on which to model the managerial role.

First, it is useful to consider the distinction between role and position. Whatever managers do – or should do – it must be remembered that absolutely inherent in management is the notion of authority which stems, largely, from the position itself. Managers not only have activities and tasks to complete, but also have to take responsibility and they have to represent their organization, or their section of it. They exist within structures of authority, and have to exercise authority. This is very clear in Mintzberg's list of managerial roles, where many of the roles are directly concerned with these aspects.

Mintzberg (1980: 166) is particularly concerned with this aspect of management and accords it prime importance:

> The manager is that person in charge of a formal organization or one of its sub-chapters. He is vested with formal authority over his organizational chapter, and this leads to his two most basic purposes. First, the manager must ensure that his organization produces its specific goods or services efficiently. . . . Second, the manager must ensure that his organization serves the ends of those persons who control it.

But as well as exercising power and responsibility, managers also have a series of horizontal areas over which power is exercised, for which they are responsible, and within which they must deploy the appropriate competences. Again there are various ways in which these areas can be classified and defined. We may distinguish, for example: the commercial or business area – i.e. ensuring profit, or achieving agreed levels and quality of output – the technical, when appropriate (sales, marketing, finance, personnel; and the managerial.

The MCI usefully distinguishes between: managing operations; managing finances; managing information; and managing people. It is this last aspect – managing people – which constitutes the subject matter of this book. This is the essence of management.

The fundamental task of management, as Drucker insists, is 'to make people capable of joint performance by giving them common goals, common values, the right structure, and the ongoing training and development they need to perform and to respond to change'. But he continues: 'the very meaning of this task has changed, if only because the performance of management has converted the workforce from one composed largely of unskilled labourers to one of highly educated knowledge workers' (Drucker, 1988: 75–6). These qualities – and this conception of the manager's role – are also inherent in some of the writings on competence. However, what differentiates the approaches of Boyatzis and Drucker is that Drucker specifically and explicitly isolates and emphasizes these qualities as part of his unashamed conceptually driven approach; while Boyatzis simply records them in his research-based list as important, along with others. Boyatzis, on the basis of his research alone, cannot say *why* these qualities are important. To do this he must rely on his own conception of the relationship between competence, the five basic management functions, and aspects of the organizational environment. Within the Boyatzis model there is an implicit and unresolved tension between the research findings, which are based on the views, assessments and world-views of managers, and the views and assessments of Boyatzis himself. There is no reason in principle why these two elements should be consistent with each other, despite Boyatzis's efforts to force them together. It is certainly true to say, as Boyatzis remarks, that the demands made of a person in a management job arise from the 'functional requirements' of the job. It is also true that performing these effectively will require certain skills or competences. But while the competences are derived from managers' views, the functions are derived from Boyatzis himself. The managers may have held different views of key management functions; the observer might identify different competences.

Drucker's (1988) conceptual analysis of the nature of management is useful:

> Finally, what is management? Is it a bag of techniques and tricks? A bundle of analytical tools like those taught in business schools? These are important, to be sure, just as the thermometer and a knowledge of anatomy are important to the physician. But what the evolution and history of management – its successes as well as its problems – teach is that management is, above all else, a very few, essential principles. To be specific:
>
> 1 Management is about human beings. Its task is to make people capable of joint performance, to make their strengths effective and their weaknesses irrelevant. This is

what organization is all about, and it is the reason that management is the critical, determining factor. These days, practically all of us are employed by managed institutions, large and small, business and non-business – and that is especially true for educated people. We depend on management for our livelihoods and our ability to contribute and achieve. Indeed, our ability to contribute to society at all usually depends as much on the management of the enterprises in which we work as it does on our own skills, dedication, and effort.

2 Because management deals with the integration of people in a common venture, it is deeply embedded in culture. What managers do in West Germany, in Britain, in the United States, in Japan, or in Brazil is exactly the same. How they do it may be quite different. Thus one of the basic challenges managers in a developing country face is to find and identify those parts of their own tradition, history, and culture that can be used as building blocks. The difference between Japan's economic success and India's relative backwardness, for instance, is largely explained by the fact that Japanese managers were able to plant important management concepts in their own cultural soil and make them grow. Whether China's leaders can do the same – or whether their great tradition will become an impediment to the country's development – remains to be seen.

3 Every enterprise requires simple, clear, and unifying objectives. Its mission has to be clear enough and big enough to provide a common vision. The goals that embody it have to be clear, public, and often reaffirmed. We hear a great deal of talk these days about the 'culture' of an organization. But what we really mean by this is the commitment throughout an enterprise to some common objective and common values. Without such commitment there is no enterprise; there is only a mob. Management's job is to think through, and exemplify those objectives, values, and goals.

4 It is also management's job to enable the enterprise and each of its members to grow and develop as needs and

opportunities change. This means that every enterprise is a learning and teaching institution. Training and development must be built into it on all levels – training and development that never stop.

5 Every enterprise is composed of people with different skills and knowledge doing many different kinds of work. For that reason it must be built on communication and on individual responsibilities. Each member has to think through what he or she aims to accomplish – and make sure that associates know and understand that aim. Each has to think through what he or she owes to others and make sure that others understand and approve. Each has to think through what is needed from others – and make sure that others know what is expected of them.

6 Neither the quantity of output nor the bottom line is by itself an adequate measure of the performance of management and enterprise. Market standing, innovation, productivity, development, people, quality, financial results – all are crucial to a company performance and indeed to its survival. In this respect, an enterprise is like a human being. Just as we need a diversity of measures to assess the health and performance of a person, we need a diversity of measures for an enterprise. Performance has to be built into the enterprise and its management; it has to be measured – or at least judged – and it has to be continuously improved.

7 Finally, the single most important thing to remember about an enterprise is that there are no results inside its walls. The result of business is a satisfied customer. The result of a hospital is a healed patient. The result of a school is a student who has learned something and puts it to work ten years later. Inside an enterprise, there are only cost centres. Results exist only on the outside.

At this stage in the analysis, for purposes of this book, it is necessary to focus specifically and clearly on the *management* aspects of the management role. This means separating off aspects of the managerial role which focus on the responsibilities of, or the exercise of, formal hierarchical authority. The focus of this book is on managing – and managing means managing other people.

What, though, is the management of people, and what skills does it require? Management means getting things done, or, as Boyatzis (1982: 60) says: 'At the core of every manager's job is the requirement to make things happen towards a goal consistent with a plan'. Furthermore, he sensibly notes:

Although the specific types of goal and plans for which the manager is responsible may vary, every manager has some degree of responsibility for establishing goals and developing plans for achieving those goals. . . . It is the competencies in the goal and action management cluster that will enable a manager to perform these tasks effectively.

(Boyatzis, 1992: 263)

But there is a crucial element lacking here: management is not just a matter of getting things done, but involves getting things done *with and through others*.

Stripped to its essentials, management *per se*, is an inherently social activity – it requires the cooperation of others, depends on the activities of others. You cannot, by definition manage alone. What sorts of skills are likely to be necessary for managing the work of others? And what ultimately does this mean? Clearly the skills we are considering here are interpersonal or interactive skills – they are to do with how (and how skilfully) a manager interacts with other people. Managers themselves recognize the importance of these skills, and of these interpersonal relationships. A survey by Rackham *et al.* (1971: 73) found that between 85 and 90 per cent of managers believed that their effectiveness depended on their interaction with others.

Two observations need to be made at this point. First, it is not enough simply for managers to get things done through others, critical and difficult though it is. It is also crucial that the things that are done are the right things and that they are done properly (whatever that means in the particular and prevailing circumstances). So management is inherently concerned with the level of performance and, presumably, with achieving improvement in the level of performance – doing the right things, doing things right and then better, or learning to do new things.

This is a crucial point: if managers are not responsible for the quality of the work of their subordinates, then they are not truly managers. And by being 'responsible' we mean, simply, that to be someone's manager means to be responsible for the quality of someone else's work – if that someone else is failing, then so is the manager, who should have recognized the problem and taken appropriate action. So management is not just getting things done through others but also working with these others to ensure that they do the right things and do them well.

Second, because management involves getting things done through and with others, the focus on improvement is inherently and unavoidably interpersonal, social: it will occur within a relationship between the manager and another person. So the skills of managing performance and improvement are social skills. Management skills are the skills of achieving someone else's improvements – plus, perhaps those of the manager. Let us look at these in more detail. What is involved in getting people to do the right things, to do them right, and to help them do them better?

6

THE MANAGEMENT OF PERFORMANCE AND LEARNING

This chapter begins with an analysis of what managers need to do in order to manage well, and how they need to do it. In order to consider what needs to be done – and how – for managers to manage well, it is first necessary to consider what a successful outcome of the process of management might look like, and then build backwards, identifying the processes and behaviours which would work to produce (or not to produce) these desired outcomes. What are we trying to achieve? And how can we achieve it?

But before that we need to clarify the types of situation which is relevant here: we are considering any managerial situation where a manager wishes, in co-operation with others, to analyse a situation and produce some improvement in output or process or some good-quality solution. Such discussions will focus on problems or challenges that require solutions, on errors, or simply on issues of performance. These issues of performance need not be negative: they need not arise because of apparently 'poor' performance. These discussions will be part of a continual implementation by the manager of the major responsibility of the managerial role – to address the quality of work, and to achieve improvement in it. So the concern here is not simply or even primarily with what passes, in many organizations, for appraisal or formal performance review, but with problem-solving and performance management.

What, then, would constitute a successful outcome of such discussions – how would we decide that they had been success- ful? First, we want to produce good-quality outcomes – solutions that involve thorough analysis and reflection based on relevant and accurate data. Second, we want all parties to the discussion to be committed to the data, the analysis and the final decision, and to be clear about it. Third, we want the process itself to support the relationship between the parties and to lead to both parties' learning, and to some enhancement of the subordinate's motivation, understanding and commitment.

It is claimed in this book that the essentially *managerial* aspects of managers' work is their responsibility for monitoring and improving the work of others; their *managerial* effectiveness is determined by their capacity to improve the work of others. If managers are not able to make this contribution, then what value are they adding? The only ultimate justification of managers' existence is the improvement of the work of their subordinates. If managers fails in this they fail as managers.

When managers wish to encourage and direct members of their staff so that they are able and willing to do things differently, or to start doing new things and to stop doing some old things, the process these members of staff go through is a process of learning. In many respects, managing performance is very similar to managing learning. After all, what is learning but devising or mastering ways of doing or understanding new things or old things better? And so we are led to the conclusion that if we accept that management is getting the right things done well with and through others, then managers are centrally involved in achieving the learning of those others in whose work they are interested.

If this is the case then we must consider how learning happens. We must also consider what stages the process of learning passes through, for these will be the same stages through which managers must support their staff.

The most important preconditions for learning are four in number. First, managers must understand the dynamics and principles of adult learning, and use these skilfully. Second, managers must bring an appropriate approach to the perform-ance-focused discussion, and to the subordinate, in order to make it work; curiosity and determination to build a well-based, mutually satisfying plan of action must overwhelm any concern to punish or to prescribe a unilateral solution. Third, there must exist an appropriate relationship between the parties, which in turn requires the achievement of the appropriate type of manage-ment 'style'. Finally, managers must be able to encourage others to learn the appropriate skills.

The first three issues are dealt with below. The remainder of this chapter is concerned with the first key prerequisite. Chapter 6 considers the second and third prerequisites: how learning can be achieved, and the type of interaction or relationship within which learning may occur. The issue of skills is addressed in Chapter 9, which considers how performance management can be achieved in practice.

According to the model offered here, the first precondition for achieving learning is that it must be mutual and consensual, not unilateral and coercive. But this is still not enough. We must also address what learning is, and how it can be achieved. This is now our concern.

First, an important word of clarification. Learning is obviously focused on improvement; and this might be taken to imply that it is necessarily based on the analysis of historic data. But this is only one possibility, albeit a crucially important one. Learning can also be focused on what *might* happen. A lot of learning is anticipatory; it involves the creation of speculative data. We learn in the present on the basis of the past, and in learning invent possible futures, which we wish to create or avoid. The implication of this is that the series of stages described shortly as the learning cycle is also a description of an approach to problem-solving.

It may seem strange to suggest that managing has anything to do with learning, or even more strange, that managing actually involves, centrally, the management or achievement of others' learning. After all, managers often see themselves and the management function as characteristically concerned with the 'real' world, with facts and applications, rather than with concepts and theory.

Of course this caricatured view is simplistic. Theories are

actually highly practical; we would not get very far in our everyday, practical lives and work without the use (if implicit and unconscious) of theories. The exaggerated contrast between management as activity focused on practical outcomes and measures, and learning as concerned with playful, almost irresponsible speculation and the development of models and frameworks, fails to recognize that achieving successful, good-quality outcomes actually involves as central and key elements the development of theories and models of some sort.

Managers, however much they may claim to be focused on the real world, are, like everyone else, in the grip of theories which inform their behaviour. It is to their advantage to confront, think about and test the theories which inform their behaviour. This is the first step in learning: learning about yourself and how you think and relate to others and work and manage others. Thus learning about yourself is a first step in achieving learning in yourself and others.

In order to develop the point that managing and learning are closely related and inter-dependent, we need to look more closely at what happens when people learn.

How do managers learn?

Managers probably learn in more or less the same way as anyone else, although they will have some distinctive preferences for how, when and why they learn. So how does anyone learn?

The model of learning used here is based on the work of Kolb and Fry (1975). It applies to the relationship between learning and experience – that is, it is concerned with how people learn to behave differently within a context of experience – of actual or expected consequences. Before discussing this model, which basically identifies a number of stages which the learner moves through in a process of learning, try to work these out for yourself, in terms of your experience of learning. The following questions may help:

- What happens that makes you start learning?
- What do you need in order to learn?
- What are the stages you move through?

You need not think only of work examples. Oddly enough, people are often much more aware of the need to learn, and much more focused on improvement, in their leisure activities than they are in their work. It is not uncommon to find that people with hobbies or sporting interests are constantly concerned to improve their performance at these; yet at work the same people very rarely focus on the need constantly to improve what they do. This is curious. It suggests that there may be something about work organizations which stifles the urge to learn and improve. These barriers to learning are considered later in Chapter 8.

It is useful to establish a few basic assumptions about the nature of managerial actions. Learning involves the identification of a connection between causes and effects, with consequent alteration of what are identified (correctly or not) as the cause of the undesired or desired outcomes. Therefore, and crucially, we need to consider the relationship between managers' intentions and their behaviour. Do managers intend to do what they do?

Let us assume that when managers behave towards others in ways which are intended to produce desired outcomes, they have some idea, however vague and muddled, about these desired outcomes, and that they genuinely intend to achieve them. And let us assume that they have some expectation (however reasonable or ill founded) that the behaviour they use will produce the effects they desire.

To insist on these rather pedantic principles may seem odd, but actually they are fundamental: it is important to be sure that a manager intended (or did not intend) to achieve an effect in order to be able to help the manager understand and correct his or her behaviour when things go wrong.

If the effect was unintended, then there is an issue of what Argyris (1990) would call 'error' to address. An error is a mismatch between intention and outcome. It demonstrates the need for learning; it supplies the ground on which to build learning.

But if a manager creates a negative outcome, however dreadful, but *intended* to do so then there is no issue of error as such. The person did what was intended: that is success.

The discussion of data on performance is the essential first step in any discussion aimed at achieving improvement – the first thing to ensure is that as much information as possible is available, and is addressed. The identification and consideration of the relevant data on the events of the issue in question are the first steps in learning.

In practice, this distinction between intention and effect is often clouded by the fact that managers are unaware (deliberately or accidentally) or confused about the consequences they produce, and therefore they are unable to assess intention against outcome. They may also be unsure about the outcomes they intended. They may prefer to delude themselves about what happened. They may not have noticed what they did. They may even confuse their intentions with the results of their actions, and, when things go wrong, feel misunderstood, or choose to blame another person for excessive or inexplicable reactions: 'I was only trying to help and he . . .'.

In fact what we may find is that managers behave almost reflexively – simply behaving as they have learnt to behave in this and other managerial situations without really considering either the nature or efficiency of these means, or the exact nature of the ends they are pursuing. And they may not even know that they are doing it. Their skills may be unconscious, tacit, unconsidered and unrecognized but very overused. In fact these are almost defining qualities of established, polished skills.

It may be precisely because the analysis of outcomes forces an evaluation of the efficiency of the means used to achieve them, that such an analysis is rare: but it is highly rewarding for it requires a surfacing of deep, tacit routines and skills and assumptions. This is one reason for the difficulty in exploring and unravelling the manager's conception of actual ends and actual means; and a reason for its value. But the complexity and ambiguity of the data on managerial outcomes, coupled with the difficulties of getting at them, also contribute to the difficulties of assessing the efficiency of managerial behaviour as measured against the achievement of identified outcomes.

It is, of course, true that, as Mumford (1980: 64) notes 'a great deal of managerial behaviour is undertaken with at best unclear objectives, and with little attempt to find out how far the consequences relate to the objectives'. But it is equally clear that although this may be common, it is also ineffective and incompetent and has clear consequences: 'The result can be a form of

LIVERPOOL JOHN MOORES UNIVERSITY
LEARNING SERVICES

learning which is positively disadvantageous to effective management, that a manager "learns" from his understanding of the consequences a relationship between action and result which is in fact incorrect' (Mumford, 1980: 64–5).

So the assumption that managers engage in purposeful behaviour which in some way, and with highly variable degrees of success, is intended to achieve an identified objective (however vague or confused the objective and ill-considered the means) is central to our model of management behaviour, and indeed of learning. It would not be possible to regard management behaviour as concerned with achieving learning, or as itself involving learning, if this were not the case.

That managers are concerned with behaving in ways which achieve their ends is central, however, in two ways. In the first place, it applies to the manager who is seeking to achieve a high-quality solution or decision through interaction with others, and in this case the assumption targets the ways in which the manager chooses to work with others to achieve this output. One way of conceptualizing this is as follows: how successful was the manager at achieving his or her own learning, and/or the learning of others? In this case the purpose for which appropriate means must be selected and deployed is nothing less than the achievement of learning.

The second way in which this assumption is central applies not only to the responsibility of managers to achieve learning in others and themselves, but also to the learning process itself. What this means is that for learning to occur the learner must address the issue of the choice of ends desired (and the appropriateness of these ends), the appropriateness of the means the manager has used, the successfulness of these ends and how a superior performance (a better level of achievement of the ends) could be achieved through different means (different behaviour).

One practical implication is that much learning can be achieved by helping others – and conceivably oneself – by working through the following stages (while recognizing, as will be discussed later, that managers may find the rigorous and mechanical progression through these stages difficult):

- Obtain accurate neutral, descriptive data, on how they behaved, what they actually did.
- Consider what the implications of this behaviour were for all concerned.
- Contrasting this with what they wanted or were trying to achieve, and consider how the behaviour could be adjusted in order to achieve the objectives more effectively.
- Develop and implement a plan for performing the action differently.

So we have a series of issues that learning requires: data; implications of behaviour or data; analysis of reasons for behaviour or data; and identification of how things could be done differently. And these, of course, are the key stages of learning.

Another practical implication is that with complex work behaviour – much of it in situations involving other people, where we may invest much of our own conception of our personal worth and identity, where data on behaviour are ambiguous, even contested, and where relationships may be coloured by competition, politics and rivalry – managerial learning will be very complex, and will require a great deal of skill and a distinctive, appropriate approach.

A third implication is that in order to assist others' learning, the manager must use certain types of language and language skills – particularly, as the discussion suggested, questioning techniques.

Some examples

Some examples may help at this stage. We shall start with some hypothetical cases, but later in the book we shall ask you to analyse some real material – your own experiences of performance-focused discussions.

In the first case a manager wishes to discuss a subordinate's performance – say, a report the subordinate has written. The ends in this case are to assist the subordinate in learning about this piece of work – in helping him see how it could be improved. Note that this aim is quite different from the aim of assessing the report. Of course, in order for the subordinate to be able to consider how best to improve this piece of work it is necessary that he assess its virtues and weaknesses. But this assessment is now a part of a larger process: the achievement of learning. And an excessive focus on assessment itself could well compromise the achievement of the larger goal.

The manager's behaviour in this process of achieving learning – the means she chooses – must be judged in terms of the success of the actions in producing the desired effect of learning in the subordinate. If the subordinate can be brought to recognize qualities of the report he had not noticed before, if he sees how these might have implications for the reader he had not thought about, if he sees ways in which the report might be more successful in whatever terms he might use to judge this, if these criteria themselves have now been more thoroughly reviewed and possibly adjusted, and if he is committed to a way of making changes he can recognize and sees how he might achieve them, then the interaction can be described as successful. If, on the other hand, the subordinate feels bruised, depressed, inadequate, confused, with no clear plan, no understanding of the report's faults or strengths, then the session has failed. If the session has failed our interest in the matter changes. Now we are interested not simply in why it has failed (though we are interested in this and will consider it) but in whether and how the manager herself is going to consider her own performance – her behaviour in terms of her objectives.

The key question now is whether or not the manager has learnt that she has not succeeded and whether she is capable of managing her own learning to look into the grounds for this mismatch. In order to assist her in this it would, of course, be necessary to help her think about exactly the same issues as she should have addressed with the subordinate – to consider what she was trying to do, how she would judge the success of the session, to consider what she knows about the subordinate's feelings at the end of the session, to evaluate how well the discussions identified strengths and weaknesses and their causes, and so on. Thus the model and process of learning are applied to learning itself.

In the second case the relationship between ends and means is central to and part of the process of learning itself. That is, by

JOHN MOORES UNIVERSITY
TRUEMAN STREET LIBRARY
TEL. 051 231 4022/4023

considering what the manager was trying to do, and how far and in what ways it was achieved, the manager considers his performance and how it could be improved. What he must do – with his manager's assistance if he is lucky – is assess what the objectives of the piece of work were and how far was he successful. This means that he must think about his work, identify clearly and accurately its various qualities, and consider the implications of these qualities for the impact of the report on the relevant audiences. These implications must be assessed in terms of a view of how strengths could be supported and weaknesses overcome: the process should identify possible ways in which the work, were it to be done again, could be improved.

The experiential approach to learning, which underlies the view of learning and of management as the management of performance improvement, focuses on analytical cognitive processes as central elements in the learning process. That is, it identifies the stages we go through when we learn from experience within the context of some desired objective.

Kolb's approach, as Mumford (1980: 66) notes argues that learning and development are achieved by an integrated process that is firmly based on experience and consists of the following stages:

- Concrete experience: starts with the collection of data and observation.
- Reflective observation: moves to an analysis of the implications of these data – observing, analysing, thinking about the data.
- Abstract conceptualization: generates abstract concepts and models, constructing patterns and models.
- Active experimentation: results in actions intended to maximize desired effects and to test the model.

This model (Figure 6.1) is fundamental to the view of managerial effectiveness used in this book. It has a number of key elements which are valuable for our purposes.

- It shows learning as a cyclical process, with integrated stages impacting on each other serially and logically, and with each cycle leading always to new cycles. The process never stops. The action of one sweep of the process produces data for another sweep; each end is a beginning.

LIVERPOOL
JOHN MOORES UNIVERSITY
TRUEMAN STREET LIBRARY
TEL. 051 231 4022/4023

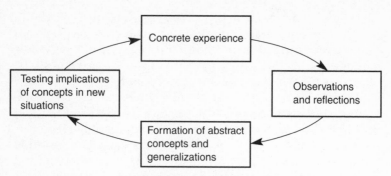

Figure 6.1 The learning cycle
Source: Kolb and Fry (1975)

- Learning is placed in the context of everyday life and experience – it is not regarded as something that happens only in explicit and formal 'learning' or 'training' sessions.
- It is argued that individuals vary in their individual preference for, and personal emphasis on, different stages in the learning cycle. These preferences are reasonably constant and reliable, although they can be modified over time and with effort. Kolb calls these preferences 'learning styles'.

Kolb (1984, quoted in Mumford, 1980: 77) writes: 'As a result of our hereditary equipment, our particular past life experience and the demands of our present environment, most people develop learning styles that emphasise some learning abilities over others.'

A preference for any one of the four positions on the learning cycle means that a person learns best and most from that stage of the cycle, and may find the other stages distasteful or difficult. Kolb's original research into the patterning of managers' learning preferences found four statistically prevalent learning styles, each of which involved a preference for a combination of two learning positions. However, research into learning styles is now dominated by a broadly similar typology developed by Honey and Mumford (1986). These authors identify four learning styles, each one associated with a preference for a stage of the learning cycle:

Activists
Activists involve themselves fully and without bias in new experiences. They enjoy the here and now and are happy to

72

be dominated by immediate experiences. They are open-minded, not sceptical, and this tends to make them enthusiastic about anything new. Their philosophy is: 'I'll try anything once'. They tend to act first and consider the consequences afterwards. Their days are filled with activity. They tackle problems by brainstorming. As soon as the excitement from one activity has died down they are busy looking for the next. They tend to thrive on the challenge of new experiences but are bored with implementation and longer-term consolidation. They are gregarious people constantly involving themselves with others but, in doing so, they seek to centre all activities around themselves.

Reflectors
Reflectors like to stand back to ponder experiences and observe them from many different perspectives. They collect data, both first hand and from others, and prefer to think about them thoroughly before coming to any conclusion. The thorough collection and analysis of data about experiences and events is what counts so they tend to postpone reaching definitive conclusions for as long as possible. Their philosophy is to be cautious. They are thoughtful people who like to consider all possible angles and implications before making a move. They prefer to take a back seat in meetings and discussions. They enjoy observing other people in action. They listen to others and get the drift of the discussion before making their own points. They tend to adopt a low profile and have a slightly distant, tolerant, unruffled air about them. When they act it is part of a wide picture which includes the past as well as the present and others' observations as well as their own.

Theorists
Theorists adapt and integrate observations into complex but logically sound theories. They think problems through in a vertical, step-by-step logical way. They assimilate disparate facts into coherent theories. They tend to be perfectionists who will not relax until things are tidy and fit into a rational scheme. They like to analyse and synthesize. They are keen on basic assumptions, principles, theories models and

systems thinking. Their philosophy prizes rationality and logic. 'If it's logical it's good'. Questions they frequently ask are: 'Does it make sense?' 'How does this fit with that?' 'What are the basic assumptions?' They tend to be detached, analytical and dedicated to rational objectivity rather than anything subjective or ambiguous. Their approach to problems is consistently logical. This is their 'mental set' and they rigidly reject anything that does not fit with it. They prefer to maximize certainty and feel uncomfortable with subjective judgements, lateral thinking and anything flippant.

Pragmatists

Pragmatists are keen on trying out ideas, theories and techniques to see if they work in practice. They positively search out new ideas and take the first opportunity to experiment with applications. They are the sort of people who return from management courses brimming with new ideas that they want to try out in practice. They like to get on with things and act quickly and confidently on ideas that attract them. They tend to be impatient with ruminating and open-ended discussions. They are essentially practical, down-to-earth people who like making practical decisions and solving problems. They respond to problems and opportunities 'as a challenge'. Their philosophy is: 'There is always a better way' and 'If it *works* it's good'.

It is worth while considering the implications of people's variations in learning styles, for these can be important. First, they touch on how we prefer to learn. We will use (and probably overuse) our preferred approach. For example, pragmatists will be keen to get on and try out new ideas, and less keen on discussions about possibilities and options. Pragmatists may find 'abstract' discussion irrelevant and frustrating. They may have a strong need for clear guidelines and lessons; ambiguity will be hard for them. Understanding your own learning style therefore is useful in helping you understand your own learning resistances and preferences.

Second, variations in learning styles are also important in helping you understand the difficulties you may have when helping others learn. It is likely, after all, that we try to help others learn in the same way that we learn ourselves – for this will seem natural to us. So theorists will focus attention on the theory or model involved in the process; they address, and encourage others to address, the assumptions and logic of the process. They will give less attention and less value, to speedy decision-making, or to issues of practical relevance – issues of much greater importance to pragmatists.

Try to identify your own learning style. There are question-naires available to help you do this. But for our purposes here it is enough if you simply identify your preference from the descriptions above. Now consider the following questions:

1 What are the implications of your 'learning style' for the way you manage others, and particularly for the way you try to help them improve their performance?
2 What are the implications of your 'learning style' for the ways you interact with others at your place of work?
3 Our learning style gives some indication of how we learn; it also shows how we try to influence others – by approaching them in the way we like to be approached. Are there any interesting implications here for you about how you typically try to influence others?

It was suggested earlier that managers probably learn like anyone else, and this is presumably true in that managers use the same basic processes as others when they learn. However, earlier discussions of the nature of management work – the short cycles of activity, the large numbers of activity sequences, the emphasis on action and being busy, etc. – suggest that managers may learn in particular ways, or may have preferences for particular positions within the learning cycle. An obvious possibility is that they may, for example, prefer action-focused learning. Managers often seem to prefer action to reflection, or data gathering to analysis.

Some have interpreted these preferences as indicating that managers do not actually spend much time thinking: 'managers seem to act thoughtfully, but spend no time thinking' (Weick, 1983: 221). But Weick also remarks that just because managers do not seem to spend time thinking in ways that are easily recognized by observers, it is not necessarily the case that they do not think. It may be that the observers are looking for the wrong thing. For managers, thinking and action coexist. Managers may not use the linear (or cyclical) stage models of thinking, or may work through them extremely quickly, using well-practised mental routines very skilfully. Managers are unlikely to spend long periods away from activity, in solitary, silent undistracted reflection (and if they did they might find themselves on the receiving end of some robust feedback!). Yet for managers, argues Weick (1983: 222) 'thinking is inseparably woven into and occurs simultaneously with action'. Managers, Weick argues, *behave thinkingly*.

There are some interesting implications of this argument. The most serious one is that encouraging managers to think in a series of successive steps may encounter resistance from some. Yet while the notion of a series of sequential stages or steps may not fit in with managers' preferred ways of thinking, the steps themselves are still valid and important. The point is not that managers' thinking does not and should not involve data collection, reflection, etc., but that these steps *may occur simultaneously* rather than sequentially:

> At a given moment, one of the four may be more salient, but three others are commonly being done and may occur in a different order . . . we should pay more attention to simultaneity of thought and action and less attention to sequence.
>
> (Weick, 1983: 240–1)

Thus any effort to encourage performance improvement (learning) must attend to the stages of learning but be tolerant of non-academic models and sequences of management thinking.

Our understanding of adult learning has been enhanced by the work of Rogers (1986). He noted that adult learning tends to have four characteristics. First, it is usually episodic in character, occurring in short bursts of intense activity. Second, the learning goal is usually a specific, concrete, immediate and important task. Third, adults tend to adopt particular learning styles or strategies. Finally, learning efforts are focused on the immediate and short term (Salaman and Batsleer, 1994, from Rogers, 1986: 68–71). This model of adult learning shows some clear connections with the analysis of management work, discussed earlier. Clearly any attempts to support management learning must attend to the distinctive ways in managers, as adults, learn.

7

ACHIEVING LEARNING

This is the crux of the matter. Management *per se* involves producing improved performance in self and others: this can only be achieved by the complete and thorough progress of all the parties concerned through the stages of the learning cycle, in order to produce good-quality solutions and outcomes to which both parties are committed. How can this be achieved? How can managers assist and support the progress of others through the learning cycle?

Before starting a discussion of how this might be done effectively, let us start with some data on how you would do it. Imagine that you are about to initiate a discussion with a subordinate about his work. The subordinate is able, enthusiastic and usually reasonably effective. But over the last few months his work has deteriorated. There have been complaints from some clients; some of his colleagues have made references to things he has done or said that concern you. You have tried to raise this matter before but the subordinate has brushed the matter away by insisting that everything is OK. Things in fact seem to be growing worse.

How would you start this discussion? Try writing down the actual words you would use, and how the subordinate might react. What are your objectives in this discussion? What 'strategy' will you follow? How would you evaluate the success of the discussion?

Discussions like these are extremely difficult. One problem is that the way we approach the discussion, although genuinely informed by the desire for a successful outcome, may actually make the situation worse. For all that we may tread warily, trying to avoid offence or the appearance of attack, the subordinate senses that something odd is going on and therefore reacts warily, which we notice and which confirms our concern that the subordinate might be 'defensive'. Furthermore as this cycle of mutually supporting anxiety and avoidance develops, it is also denied overtly by the participants, which further fuels suspicion.

Another aspect of such discussions is that they require considerable communicative skill. One reason why managers find them difficult is that they try to resolve them in the same way as they resolve technical, professional matters – by being right, by informing, instructing, selling, persuading, by calculations and application of principles, etc. These skills do not work here: they lead, in fact, to a paradox that we call *trained incompetence* – the misapplication of skills outside the area of their relevance. We need to identify the skills that are pertinent here.

Much has already been said in this book concerning how performance-focused discussions should be handled. For example, a contrast must be drawn between an open, joint process of analysis and discussion, involving both parties, and a one-way, authoritarian and imposed approach. The deficiencies of the latter are many: not only does it depend entirely on the omniscient manager having a monopoly on information, analysis, ideas, options and decisions (a relatively rare occurrence): but also it fails on the second key criterion by which we define success – achieving the commitment of all parties to the solution and action decisions.

An open, public process of analysis, exploration and decision-making can only be achieved by means of appropriate language skills, and these will be discussed in some detail later on. But at this stage we need to explore more thoroughly the process overall.

The effective approach to achieving performance improvement proceeds through a set of key stages – the stages of the learning cycle – in a process that is joint, mutual and open. The stages have already been considered: data, reflection, theory and action. But they need development. Essentially, discussions focused on performance involve a series of questions organized around some simple and obvious steps:

- *Data*. What happened? What data are available? If the relevant data are not available, are not agreed, discussed, or if disagreements are not aired, then progress is impossible. You might find that in many conversations, it is differences on data that constitute the major problem. In this case the problem shifts from the original issue to one of considering how the disagreement can be resolved.
- *Reflection*. What does this mean? What are the implications? What went well/badly? What did you intend? What did others intend? What did they make of what happened? What assumptions were made and by whom? What models of behaviour were in use?
- *Theory*. How could things be done better? What are the options? What are the consequences. What if . . . ? Why did that happen?
- *Action*. What shall be done by whom, when and how?

This list is by no means exhaustive, but is simply intended to illustrate the content of the discussions at each stage of the cycle. Another way of seeing the stages is in terms of the following:

- *Position*. What do we know about the existing state of affairs?
- *Problem*. The issues, implications, meaning of this situation.
- *Possibilities*. Possible options and solutions based on our analysis and understanding.
- *Proposal*. Selection and activation of preferred option with analysis of risks, costs, key contingencies, environmental and other dependences.

But just as important as the stages of learning is the appropriate approach or method adopted by the parties to ensure open, explicit and reflexive discussion and analysis. This is difficult to achieve. While managers frequently claim that they wish to achieve learning, and often mean what they say, their practices belie their intentions: their 'espoused' theory which describes

Table 7.1 Practical implications of how managers learn

Feature	Implications for managers and trainers
1 Episodic, not continuous	Rely on short bursts of learning activity Break material into manageable units, rather than hook each one on to other items of learning
2 Goal, task and problem-centred	Make relevant to learners' needs and motivation Be aware of learners' intentions Learners to set goals Start where they are – not necessarily the beginning Do activity now, rather than prepare for it in the future
3 Learning styles and strategies	Be aware of different learning styles; build up learning skills
• Analogical thinking; use of existing knowledge and experience	Relate new material and skills to existing experience and knowledge Be sensitive to range and use of experience
• Trial and error	Discovery learning; learner needs to be active, not passive recipient Need for reinforcement; build in feedback Need for practice
• Meaningful wholes	Move from simplified wholes to more complex wholes Help to built up units to create whole; select out essential from non-essential units
• Less memory; demonstration and imitation	Rely on understanding for retention – not memory Use of demonstration
4 Lack of interest in general principles	Move from concrete to general, not from general to concrete; encourage questioning of general principles; build up relationships Remotivate to further learning

Source: adapted from Rogers (1986: 74).

what they value and intend is undermined by their 'theory in use' which articulates other priorities. The source of this discrepancy is not necessarily hypocrisy – it is more likely to be lack of skill.

Table 7.1 lists some practical implications of the ways in which managers learn.

Analysis of how managerial learning can be achieved has been enormously influenced by the work of Chris Argyris. Argyris identified the capacity to learn on the part of managers, and consequently, organizations, as absolutely fundamental to organizational effectiveness. He also notes a number of pervasive blockages and limitations to learning as endemic and systemic within organizations. These are considered in Chapter 8.

Argyris starts his analysis with a paradox. He refers to research by Beer *et al.* (1988) into the consequences of change programmes in a number of organizations. Their research reported that each company 'had managed itself into an uncompetitive position'. Beer *et al.* found that within each company there were:

- inflexible and unadaptive rules;
- managers and workers out of touch with customer needs;
- managers who were not committed, not co-operative, and often not competent to produce change;
- poor interaction among functional groups;
- top management refusing to believe that lower revenues and market share were more than a temporary perturbation;
- lack of strategic thinking;
- lower-level employees not fully informed;
- low levels of trust.

Furthermore, Beer *et al.* (1988) noted that the change pro-grammes initiated in the organizations seemed to run up against the very problems they were intended to overcome, so the programmes seemed to fade away. This raises the key question, for Argyris and for this book:

Why is it that well-educated and well-intentioned managers, at all levels, produced these policies and practices? . . . Why is it that managers . . . take for granted policies and practices that are contrary to their managerial stewardship [and] by-pass root causes? They equate being realistic with being simplistic. They make all these actions undiscussable. They thus wind up creating a world in which the bad is tied up with the good so that producing the latter guarantees the former.

(Argyris 1990: 5–6)

There are two puzzles here, both of which are central to difficulties that occur in achieving learning even when people intend to achieve learning. First, 'why do human beings produce, adhere to and proliferate errors when we know that they did not (and indeed could not) intend them?' (ibid.: 9). Second, why is it that people apparently work hard to produce errors (undesired consequences of their actions), and find it difficult to stop producing them? For the ultimate paradox is not that managers consistently produce results they do not intend, but that they continue to produce them. When things go wrong they continue to go wrong and the attempts to explore and redress them go wrong.

The problem identified by Argyris is the problem identified in this book. It is that of identifying the importance of learning within organizations, why it does not happen and what is necessary for it to occur.

Argyris distinguishes two approaches to the achievement of learning. The first, which he calls model I, is essentially the approach described earlier: top-down, controlled and controlling, dominated by the senior management with respect to information, evaluation and prescription. He usefully identifies three components of error-focused discussion: advocacy (what should be done; what is necessary and valuable and possible etc.); evaluation (judging, appraising), and attribution (attributing meanings and values and opinions to others). He argues that discussions of performance and error will always include these three elements; but the thing that distinguishes model II discussions from model I discussions is that with model II these processes are open, and tested and testable – this is the difference between model I and model II – i.e. in our terms between an approach which is top-down dominated and one which is open and exploratory, enquiring and testing nature. As Argyris puts it, in model II participants approach the learning experience not with frustration, shame, fear and embarrassment, but with excitement and curiosity, and the way they work together articulates this approach. Errors, disasters, and performance issues now become not crimes to cover up or prosecute, but puzzles to be analysed and considered. The manager role is thus no longer a policing function, but a learning function. This is achieved by across-the-board openness; the constituent learning strategies are as follows:

- Make reasoning (including the data on which it is based) public and testable.
- Initiate experiments and lines of enquiry.
- Publicly reflect on reactions to these.

If, in the process of discussion, things go wrong (and they will) then these new order errors themselves should be discussable, becoming in their turn the new focus of enquiry, the new problem. Here the strategies are the same – public identification, enquiry and reflection. But the process occurs at another level – it is second-order meta-learning, where the object of enquiry is error in the learning process itself.

For reasons which we will discuss later, it is difficult to master these skills in practice, although relatively easy to comprehend and accept them intellectually. But the objective of the approach is precisely the same as that identified as the objective of the competent manager: the identification and analysis of error, and thus the achievement of improvement in learning. Argyris sees this in terms of three governing values. These bear a strong similarity to the desired outcome of collective, mutual progress through the stages of the learning cycle. They are as follows:

- Seek information and validate it.
- Promote free and informed choice (options, decisions).
- Ensure commitment to the decision.

This nicely encapsulates the stages and elements of any learning situation and supplies useful criteria by which to judge the success of a learning intervention.

However, if learning is essential to management, and if management consists of the achievement of learning, then how far and in what ways might the organizational context facilitate or obstruct the achievement of learning? These are the concerns of the following two chapters.

8

BARRIERS TO LEARNING

Our prevailing system of management has destroyed our people.
People are born with intrinsic motivation, self-esteem, dignity,
curiosity to learn, joy in learning. The forces of destruction begin
with toddlers – a prize for the best Hallowe'en costume, grades in
school, gold stars, and on up through the university. On the job,
people, teams, divisions are ranked – reward for the one at the top,
punishment at the bottom. MBO, quotas, incentive pay, business
plans, put together separately, division by division, cause further
loss, unknown and unknowable.

(Deming, quoted in Senge, 1990: 7)

Superior performance, argues Senge, depends on superior
learning. If the job of managers is to manage the learning
(performance improvement) of their staff, then what sorts of
factor in the organization, or even in the individual, might
obstruct the achievement of learning? In this chapter we consider
the nature of such barriers.

It is increasingly common for business consultants, academics
and managers to argue that in order to achieve competitive edge
in a highly competitive business environment, it is necessary to
unleash and tap the energy, intelligence creativity and enthusi-
asm of staff.

Bureaucracy is giving way to new approaches that require people exercise discretion, take initiatives, and assume a much greater responsibility for their own organisation and management. The need to remain open and flexible demands creative responses from every quarter, and many leading organisations recognise that human intelligence and the ability to unleash and direct that intelligence are critical resources.

(Morgan, 1988: 56)

But it seems that it is easier to say this than to achieve it. Despite the widespread acceptance of this requirement, Morgan (1988: 54) notes: 'Many of our organisations have difficulty doing their best. Though they show considerable promise (or promises?), they fall short in their action.' Morgan's solution to this puzzle is to advocate what he calls the skills in remote management – put simply, managers should learn to let go.

Our view is that this is not the whole answer – or even part of the answer. It simply redescribes the problem. Of course some management activities should be relinquished, and others developed. And managers should learn to encourage and allow their staff to take responsibility, and learn how to do properly the things they are responsible for. But neither is this the answer to the key question: why do managers find it hard to encourage learning, both in themselves and in others?

At the simplest level it could be argued that the reason why managers find this difficult is that they have not been exposed to the sorts of argument and definition presented in this book about the nature of management, the essentials of the manager's role, the importance of appropriate management style, of the learning cycle as a model of the learning process, etc. This is certainly very important, for knowing, understanding and accepting the conception of management presented in this book, and appreciating what is necessary to achieve it, are critical. But the problem is not simply one of ignorance or confusion. If there are things that managers must learn, there are also things that managers must *unlearn* before they can learn. Later we will see how managers have been trained and rewarded to behave in ways which are, in our terms, managerially incompetent. Furthermore, this incompetence is often unconscious, spontaneous and highly skilful.

But the barriers to learning are more fundamental than issues of mere understanding and knowledge; they go to the heart of aspects of organization itself.

Cressey and Jones, in an analysis of processes of change in a bank they call Britbank, describe the structure and culture of the bank before the process of change was designed and initiated. Their remarks are highly pertinent to our concerns here.

> In the bank's previous bureaucratic organisation staff were highly stratified by grade and work role, hierarchical in their structure, with narrow tasks for an army of mainly administrative processors of data; paper shifters with attitudes marked by deference, caution and loyalty to a primarily paternalist employer.
>
> (Cressey and Jones, 1992: 70)

They contrast this with the reformed structure:

> The new model demands quite different staff, with different qualities and outlooks. It requires an organisational culture change from one of cautious trusteeship towards a profit-centred, performance-oriented enterprise.
>
> (Cressey and Jones, 1992: 70–1)

In our terms, the first type of organization is unlikely to encourage learning, discussion, communication, analysis. The second one, if it can be achieved, is more likely to do so.

Organizations, then, can be anti-learning. Even with today's fashion for flatter, decentralized structures organizations remain hierarchical and differentiated. People still inhabit roles which, *inter alia*, differ in functional specialization and in power. Power in organizations is still centralized and unevenly distributed. These differences supply the terrain on which political behaviour grows – behaviour which seeks to protect or advance personal or sectoral advantage or security. A clear possibility of functional and hierarchical differentiation is that specialisms will seek to defend their conceptions of the organization's goal, their view of their contribution, their view of the importance of various organizational activities. As members of organizations compete for scarce rewards, in the same way departments and sections seek to defend their share of budgets, their interests, their views, their skill and resource base. Trainers are unlikely to argue for the irrelevance of training, accounts to suggest that financial controls are stifling, or marketeers to maintain that marketing is over-valued guesswork.

A consequence of the inevitable sectionalism of large organizations is that information itself (central to learning) becomes a resource which can be used to protect or to advance sectoral interest.

> Each service, each division, indeed every subunit, becomes a guardian of its own mission, standards and skills: lines of organisation become lines of loyalty and secrecy. In industry, the Personnel department defends its control over selection and training; Accounting, its standards of reporting; Production, its schedules of output; Sales, its interests in product design and customer service – each restricting information that might advance the competing interests of the others.
>
> (Wilensky, 1967: 48)

Furthermore, power within organizations can follow not simply from formal position, but also from control over some critical organizational uncertainties. Knowledge and information can thus be a source of power. It follows from this that learning, which may breach some of these citadels of private knowledge, may also breach sectoral power. Thus managers may resist learning, with all its implications for change and innovation, for two related reasons – because they fear that the identified change may have implications for their sectoral advantage, and because they may be distrustful of those who initiate the change and the learning. Under these conditions learning ceases to be a neutral process and becomes a politicized process whereby new knowledge, systems and techniques are viewed suspiciously, even rejected because they are seen to represent the priorities and views of others whose priorities are distinct, and possibly opposed, or to result in a reallocation of organizational resources or a weakening of a section's historical power base.

For example, in the old days of quantified appraisal schemes when managers were required to complete appraisals on their staff, many managers, when undergoing training in appraisal interviewing, showed a marked reluctance to learn the new skills and accept the schemes themselves. Their 'resistance' was nothing to do with their learning styles or their capacity to learn; it was based on their conviction that this sort of performance appraisal would damage their relations with their subordinates, would reduce their ability to get the best for their people and would thus result in a loss of control over staff. Personnel were frequently seen as having their own priorities and values: imposing personnel systems throughout the organization, formalizing (and thus monitoring and controlling) management, gathering data on staff performance for the personnel department's use. Managers often saw that information about their staff's performance had political significance.

Similarly, Janis (1982) argues that when a small group of managers develop strong bonds of loyalty and cohesion, and a strong interest in a particular policy or point of view (which is usually seen to be supported by the senior manager), they become victims of what Janis calls 'groupthink'. The elements of this condition are that loyalty and consensus become overriding objectives for individuals. Questioning, doubting, identifying dangers, all become evidence of disloyalty, of not being one of the team, of 'rocking the boat'. Members become blind and deaf to any data which do not support the emergent and favoured line. The group is quite unable to learn, in the sense that solidarity and commitment block the group's capacity to assess the likely outcome of its policies. When the policies fail the group often cannot accept the validity of the data which show failure.

This may be an extreme phenomenon, but it is certainly frequently the case that senior management teams have difficulty accepting that learning needs to happen, and even more difficulty in managing the learning process. Consider for example, a case in your organization where something has very obviously gone wrong – a lost account, an unsuccessful acquisition,or whatever. Is there evidence that those involved in the decision recognized that this situation required review in order to ensure that the necessary learning took place? Was reaction to the event one of curiosity, review and analysis, or of cover-up and avoidance? Were lessons identified? Were they the correct ones, in your view? If your analysis of this episode suggests that learning was not encouraged or did not take place, then what were the origins of the avoidance and cover-up, and what were the implications?

An example of how hierarchical structures can obstruct learning has been supplied by John Roberts in a useful case study. He notes:

> potential problems of learning are often . . . compounded by the routine processes of operational control. Hierarchies typically reinforce the values of conformity; to contradict a superior can be seen as a challenge to their authority, and it can seem wiser and safer to discount one's own experience and defer. This is just one of the ways in which vital knowledge is censored out of the organisation. In times of rapid change these processes are often intensified, with insecurity serving to heighten individual and group defensiveness, thereby restricting the flow of information within the company. If at this stage the hierarchy is used to impose an ill-informed strategic change, then one has created a recipe for disaster.
>
> (Roberts, 1992: 19)

Another important source of 'resistance' to learning can derive from organizational cultures. Some organizational cultures may predispose against learning by discouraging any one of the key elements that learning requires.

Paul Bate has described a number of studies of organizational change. He notes that the theory of organizational change argues that change occurs when certain preconditions are in place: a recognized problem and a determination to face and solve it, and an understanding of various courses of action and their implications. However, Bate (1992: 214) notes that even when these conditions were in place, change still did not occur. 'Something – whatever it may be – was enmeshing people in their problems in a persistent and repetitive way'.

Bate's analysis of this situation is useful because it applies closely to the subject under discussion here: barriers to learning, where a parallel process occurs. He writes:

> why were situations allowed to persist when they were accepted by the parties themselves as problematical and undesirable? Gradually a fascinating notion began to emerge that the parties were actively colluding in a process which effectively removed all possibility of a resolution to their problems . . . at the heart of this collusion process lay the organisational culture.

Bate's thesis is as follows:

> people in organisations evolve in their daily interactions with one another a system of shared perspectives of 'collectively held and sanctioned definitions of the situation' which make up the culture of these organisations. The culture once established, prescribes for its creators and inheritors certain ways of believing, thinking and acting which in some circumstances can prevent meaningful interaction and induce a situation of 'learned helplessness' – that is a psychological state in which people are unable to conceptualise their problems in such a way as to be able to resolve them. In short, attempts at problem-solving may become culture-bound.
>
> (Bate, 1992: 214)

Bate's analysis of the ways in which organizational cultures impact on members' willingness and ability to learn depends upon his view of culture as a characteristic way in which organizational members perceive and conceptualize. Culture is

> something which includes but is wider than actions, values, and norms – a conceptual structure of generalisations or contexts, postulates about what is essential, assumptions about what is valuable, attitudes about what is possible, and ideas about what will work effectively. In the organisational context this conceptual structure will encompass one's own roles, the roles of others, rules and institutions, traditional ways of acting, and specific issues such as the nature of authority, leadership and democracy . . .
>
> (Bate, 1992: 216–17)

For example, the organizational culture of an insurance brok-ing organization may be heavily imbued with the dominant business activity and values of broking – affability, relationship-building, negotiation, friendliness, the avoidance of disruption or of making waves. These may be highly appropriate in the rather closed and clubby world of the City, Lloyd's and the broking community, where underwriters and brokers work closely together and derive mutual benefit from the estab-lishment and maintenance of continuing social ties. But this culture could have negative implications for learning, for within it people find it hard to confront and deal with issues of performance; they prefer to broke solutions, or possibly to avoid the issue altogether. Competence at broking would be inversely related to competence at performance improvement – an example of skilful incompetence.

Cultures are more than mere clusters of values and attitudes, significant as these may certainly be. Cultures are also important because they define and encourage skills, habits, established 'taken-for-granted' ways of thinking and behaving. That is why it is often difficult to address culture directly and effectively: what the outsider sees clearly as an organizational culture, the man-agers simply regard as obvious, almost unconscious ways of acting. As remarked by a member of the Tigray People's Liberation Front, which we shall meet in a case study in Chapter 9: 'the fish may be the last to discover the sea'.

Therefore within the range of activities and behaviours an organizational culture identifies and recommends, staff will develop skills and habitual practices – things they do, learn to do well, and ways they learn of doing them. Cultures thus define desired skills and habit and therefore have implications for the skills and activities that are valued within an organization.

Within an engineering contracting organization, for example, it was found that the predominant and strong emphasis on facts, on hard, scientific and mechanical principles and laws, was related to consequent cultural values of certainty, clarity, pre-cision – being certain and being right. These in turn made it hard for engineers as managers to handle performance-focused dis-cussions with staff in terms of the learning cycle as described earlier. For within such discussions, when competently handled,

91

the manager must behave in a way which encourages staff to consider data, to think, to analyse (through open questioning), and must help them through all stages of the learning cycle, not just impose a set of views and suggestions. Yet the organizational culture discourages open questioning ('asking questions like this suggests you don't know the answers – managers should always know the answers!') and encourages the rapid move from the data to action on the learning cycle, because of the manager's own strongly held, and culturally valued certainties and experiences. The qualities which lead engineers to achieve management positions thus suddenly become inappropriate for these positions.

Bate's classification of key elements in organizational cultures, and their likely impact on organizational learning, is presented in the following chapter. Another useful contribution to this issue is Steele's (1977) analysis of some elements of UK cultural values and their impact on learning and change. Steele identifies certain cultural factors that could inhibit learning:

1 The value of security and stability.
2 The value of avoiding embarrassing and 'unsuitable' topics.
3 The sense of the legitimacy of hierarchical authority.
4 The emphasis on tradition and continuity.
5 A strong strain of fatalism.
6 An emphasis on rationality which leads to the rejection of new methods which are untested.

There are interesting connections between this list of cultural values and Bate's model in Chapter 9. Steele's list was devised in the mid-1970s. Things have changed very significantly since then; though the changes have frequently been difficult and painful precisely because of the existence of values like these. But the list is still useful, for even if it does not fully apply to the current situation within the UK, it still describes well some key anti-learning values. Consideration in Chapter 9 of a learning organization will show how this organization's culture radically differed from many of these values listed by Steele.

Try the following exercise: Consider the way your organization is structured (hierarchical and horizontal), the way activities are divided up and distributed, and consider the culture(s) of your organization. Finally, consider the systems and processes of selection, training and reward. Now, what are the implications, positive or negative, of these for the encouragement or achievement of learning, problem-solving, performance analysis and review? Is learning really rewarded in your organization? How?

While it is important, and sobering, to be aware of the in-built obstacles to the encouragement of learning in organizations, this does not mean that all responsibility for managers' failure to monitor and achieve improvement in the work of their subordinates can be attributed to *the* organization, *the* culture, or *the* system. However supportive or obstructive the organizational context, the individual manager is still responsible for the quality of subordinates' work. When the barriers to learning are strong, this will clearly be more difficult, but this will not alter the basic function and rationale of management. Furthermore, many of the most important obstacles to learning are not 'out there' in the organization structures and cultures, but are inside managers' minds. They are inherent in how managers define their role and responsibilities as managers, in the skills and recipes they have developed and used over the years; in the assumptions they carry about themselves and others. In fact, probably the most significant and insidious barrier to learning is the belief that it is outside forces that somehow stop each one of us from taking responsibility for achieving improvement within the area for which we are responsible.

9

THE LEARNING
ORGANIZATION

. . . the most successful corporations of the 1990s will be something called a learning organisation, a consumately adaptive enterprise.

(Fortune, quoted in Senge, 1990: 8)

Senge (1990: 8) defines his view of learning organizations as follows: 'Organisations where people continually expand their capacity to create the results they desire, where new and expansive patterns of thinking are nurtured, where collective aspiration is set free, and where people are continually learning how to learn.' In the previous chapter some major obstacles to learning were identified. In this chapter a more positive stance will be taken: what are the characteristics of organizations where learning is encouraged, where learners are admired and rewarded, where learning (and, by implication, error) is safe?

If we are advocating the importance of learning in organizations, identifying the possible barriers to and supports for learning in organizational structures and cultures is critical. We have been arguing that the central function and responsibility of managers is to monitor and assist the improvement of their own and others' performance; that effective organizations must value and encourage learning. What are the characteristics of organizational structures and cultures that promote and reward learning? Is this the same as the 'learning organization'? What would a learning organization look like?

'Learning organization' is a much used phrase. It has now become almost iconic in its symbolic status. It can mean a number of things. In practice, it often means nothing at all. One important type of definition is that offered by Senge above, who points to the ways in which members behave, think and learn within a learning organization.

Another type of definition simply conflates 'organization' and 'learning': a learning organization is one which 'facilitates the learning of all its members and continually transforms itself' (Pedler *et al.*, 1991: 25).

A third definition focuses not on individual behaviour but on organizational outcomes. This type of definition is exemplified by Pettigrew and Whipp, and discussed below.

If commitment to the 'learning organization' is now often a part of every organization's view of itself and a key slogan for most consultants, it is very much less frequently a part of its staff's practices. In these discussions it is useful to distinguish between *espoused theory* (what people say they intend and value) and *theory in action* (the actual consequences of what they do).

At an overarching level, the 'learning organization' refers to organizational qualities that are apparently much valued in today's environments and markets. At this level it is surely desirable that an organization encourages its staff to learn. After all what else could this mean?

Presumably it would mean that staff were constantly concerned with doing the right things and with doing them well (or better), and that it is the major responsibility of managers to assist the learning of others. Thus learning and helping others learn would be encouraged and the skills and practices necessary for the achievement of learning would be recognized as important.

A learning-based approach would not be focused only on individual performance issues. It would also be characteristic of problem-solving discussions, strategy discussions, etc. Any

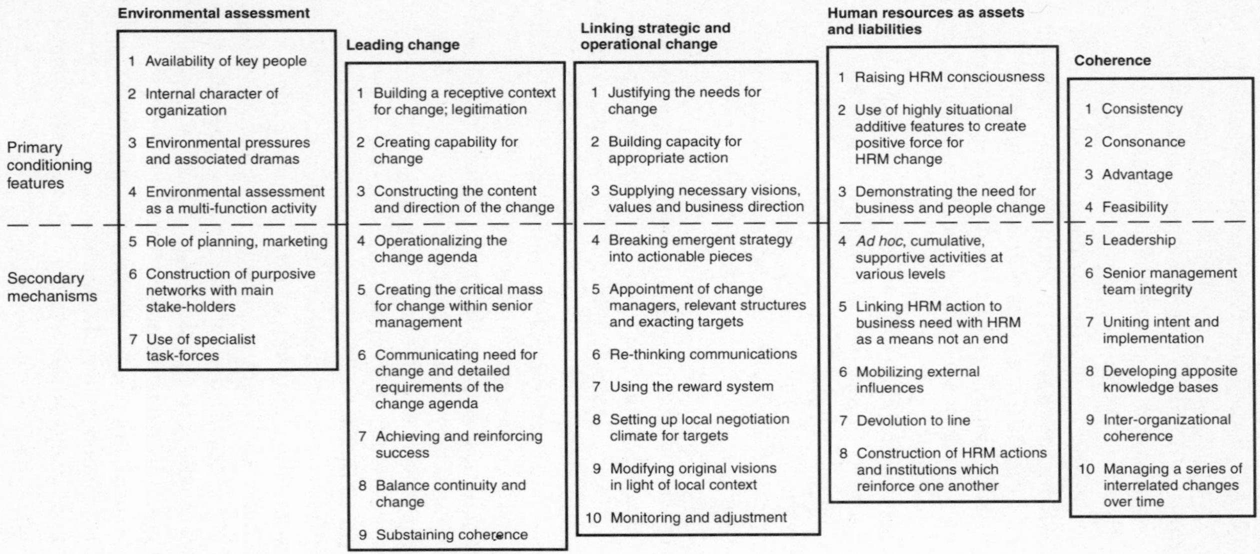

Environmental assessment

Primary conditioning features

1 Availability of key people
2 Internal character of organization
3 Environmental pressures and associated dramas
4 Environmental assessment as a multi-function activity

Secondary mechanisms

5 Role of planning, marketing
6 Construction of purposive networks with main stake-holders
7 Use of specialist task-forces

Leading change

1 Building a receptive context for change; legitimation
2 Creating capability for change
3 Constructing the content and direction of the change
4 Operationalizing the change agenda
5 Creating the critical mass for change within senior management
6 Communicating need for change and detailed requirements of the change agenda
7 Achieving and reinforcing success
8 Balance continuity and change
9 Substaining coherence

Linking strategic and operational change

1 Justifying the needs for change
2 Building capacity for appropriate action
3 Supplying necessary visions, values and business direction
4 Breaking emergent strategy into actionable pieces
5 Appointment of change managers, relevant structures and exacting targets
6 Re-thinking communications
7 Using the reward system
8 Setting up local negotiation climate for targets
9 Modifying original visions in light of local context
10 Monitoring and adjustment

Human resources as assets and liabilities

1 Raising HRM consciousness
2 Use of highly situational additive features to create positive force for HRM change
3 Demonstrating the need for business and people change
4 Ad hoc, cumulative, supportive activities at various levels
5 Linking HRM action to business need with HRM as a means not an end
6 Mobilizing external influences
7 Devolution to line
8 Construction of HRM actions and institutions which reinforce one another

Coherence

1 Consistency
2 Consonance
3 Advantage
4 Feasibility
5 Leadership
6 Senior management team integrity
7 Uniting intent and implementation
8 Developing apposite knowledge bases
9 Inter-organizational coherence
10 Managing a series of interrelated changes over time

Figure 9.1 Managing change for competitive success
Source: Pettigrew and Whipp (1991)

example of organizational analysis and thinking would, within the learning organization, be characterized by the key preconditions of learning (problem-solving approach and adult–adult relationships) and would seek good-quality, mutual solutions through progress through the stages of the learning cycle: data – reflection – theory – action.

Much recent management literature stresses the value of organizational 'flexibility' and 'responsiveness', these qualities often being related to environmental developments, particularly changes in the business environment – the increasingly competitive global nature of product markets. Under these circumstances, commentators claim, competitive advantage accrues to those businesses that develop human resource policies that 'promote continuous learning, teamwork, participation and flexibility' (Dertouzos *et al.*, 1989: 118).

Pettigrew and Whipp (1991), in a study of the ability of a number of UK firms to 'manage strategic change and to assess the outcome for competitive performance' (p. 6), conclude that a common pattern *does* emerge from the ways the firms handled strategic and operational change, and that there was an observable difference in the ways higher-performing firms managed change compared with their less successful counterparts over time (pp. 6–7). They identify five key variables: environmental assessment; leading change; linking strategic and operational change; seeing human resources as assets and liabilities; and achieving coherence. These qualities are described in Figure 9.1. They are essentially achieved via learning processes

The ability of an organization to understand the environment, for example, is obviously related to the capacity of members of the organization to gather data, reflect on them, and so on. Pettigrew and Whipp (1991: 135–6) note:

The starting point in the process of competition often derives from the understanding a firm develops of its environment. In general terms the research shows that it is insufficient for companies to regard the creation of knowledge and judgements of their external competitive world as simply a technique exercise. Rather the need is for organizations to become open learning systems. In other words, the assessment of the competitive environment does not remain the preserve of a single function nor the sole responsibility of one senior manager. Nor does it occur via isolated acts. Instead strategy creation is seen as emerging from the way a company, at various levels, acquires, interprets and processes information about its environment.

It could well be argued that the achievement of all five of these conditions requires what we would call a learning approach, as described earlier, since an underlying mechanism for the achievement of these qualities must require the generation of good-quality data, good analysis, open discussion, etc. And indeed Pettigrew and Whipp (1991: 290) argue precisely this point in their summary:

> The ability of a company to learn should be under regular scrutiny. In other words, the ability of an organisation to reconstruct and adapt its knowledge base (made up of skills, structures and values . . .) should be a key task for managers. They should also be able to apply the 'unlearning' test. In other words, is the organisation capable of mounting the creative destruction necessary to breaking down outmoded attitudes and practices, while at the same time building up new, more appropriate competences?

Finally, they add:

> If in the wake of globalisation, marketing, financial and manufacturing techniques become ever more capable of imitation, then their competitive advantage is correspondingly diminished. According to the one-time head of planning at the Royal Dutch Shell Group, in this sort of world, 'the ability to learn faster than competitors may be the sustainable advantage'.

But while these qualities – and learning itself – may be valued as outputs, as aspects of organizational members' behaviour, it is far from obvious how they may be achieved. And references to the 'learning organization' presumably refer not just to desired organizational outcomes, or to desired behaviours, but to the ways of designing or changing organizations to produce these behaviours. It is clear, for example, from Chapter 8, that many aspects of organizational structures and cultures may inhibit learning, and encourage denial, deference and defensiveness. But what would an organization have to be like for it to be a 'learning organization'? What would it take to transform this desirable but often empty notion from rhetoric into reality?

Although there has been much reference to the value of the 'learning organization', there is relatively little description of what such organizations may actually be like. Pedler *et al.* (1991: 25) have offered a list of the 'conditions' under which a learning organization can be achieved. The list includes:

- learning strategy;
- participative policy-making;
- informating (i.e. information technology used to inform and empower people to ask questions and to take decisions based on data);
- formative accounting (i.e. control systems are structured to assist learning from decisions);
- internal exchange;
- reward flexibility;
- enabling structures;
- front-line workers as environmental scanners;
- inter-company learning;
- learning climate;
- self-development for all.

This is a sensible and useful list; but needs to be fleshed out.

In order to progress this discussion of the 'learning organization', I offer below a case study of what may be just such an organization. It is an unusual organization – a military group engaged for many years in a struggle against a military dictator. Yet it may offer us a view of just what it takes to be a genuine learning organization.

Until the 1970s Ethiopia was a feudal society, with all land owned by Church, Emperor and feudal lords. The Emperor, Haile Selassie, was overthrown in 1974 by Mengistu, a Stalinist-style, Soviet-backed military dictator. He inherited an ongoing war in Eritrea which had started, when Selassie tried to crack down on democratic practices, in 1961. Mengistu initiated a frightful campaign of repression, terror and murder. In 1974 a small group of Tigrean students from Addis Ababa University left Addis Ababa and went back to Tigray. There they started small-scale resistance and political agitation. This grew into the Tigrean People's Liberation Front (TPLF). War ensued. Mengistu had the largest army in black Africa – a large airforce, tanks, helicopters and up to 100,000 troops. Seventeen years later, on 28 May 1991, the army the students had founded, plus three survivors of that group, took Addis Ababa. During the armed struggle they had had no external military support of any sort. All their arms were captured, their fighters were volunteers, and their strategy and organization self-developed.

Their success was not, they insisted, the result of their military strategy, although this has attracted a great deal of admiration from military experts, who have claimed that the final battle west of Addis Ababa, near B'hadar, was a remarkable and brilliantly planned and executed military victory. When asked about their success they answered in terms of *how* they worked, organizationally.

They fully recognized that successful achievement of objectives follows from the way in which they worked with key groups of people. Strategic success follows structure and culture if these are seen in terms of ways of relating and working.

Their key strategy was not military, but focused on a number of key relationships: of leaders among themselves; between leaders and fighters, between the army (and party) and the people, and even between the army (TPLF) and the government forces.

The army was totally and utterly dependent on the people who were, in our terms, suppliers and clients: 'We could only defeat the Dergue because we had won the support of the people.' They depended on them for food, recruits and labour. They had to work together and to pursue the same aim. So, to this end, strategy was discussed and developed with local groups, who were organized in a flat structure; errors, problems and decisions were aired and discussed with 'the people'. The fighters were constantly admonished to treat the people as their parents – to respect them and their property. This emphasis was not cosmetic; it was not what we mean by 'marketing'. It was fundamental. The TPLF leaders really do believe that their supporters (fighters and peasants) must be involved in decisions because their ideas, and their commitment, and their preparedness to sacrifice, are essential.

The focus of these relationships was *learning*. The TPLF organization placed prime emphasis on learning. This took a number of forms.

First, they developed structures and cultures which not only supported the involvement of peasants and fighters. They also allowed an open process of decision-making. For example, while key strategy decisions might be finally formulated by the leadership, the decisions would not be taken until all the leaders had initiated a series of discussions throughout the organization at all levels (including the peasants). This took time, and was obviously a security risk. Any disagreements and suggestions were brought back to the senior group and talked through until finally consensus was reached. When disagreement persisted, efforts were made to explore and resolve it. Two major possibilities were pursued: that those who disagreed knew something that the seniors did not know, in which case the leaders would, if appropriate, adjust their decision in the light of the new knowledge; or the seniors knew something the others did not, in which case they must discuss this, or demonstrate how the plan could work.

I often saw evidence of these processes. I frequently saw large numbers of soldiers moving in Addis Ababa and learnt that they were attending meetings to discuss a current issue – usually associated with demobilization. I was often told of some series of meetings with fighters or peasants about some government policy – part of the process of policy formulation. An important part of this was the emphasis on teams and team work; team skills were highly valued.

Second, they actively promoted and encouraged the value and virtue of learning. The leaders regularly held review sessions, and encouraged their colleagues to do the same. In these sessions the leaders, including the current President who was then the leader of the TPLF, would initiate proceedings by discussing things that had gone wrong for which he was responsible – his recent mistakes. It was not only safe to discuss error, it was *virtuous*. Furthermore, learning was rewarded. The military leader, now the Minister of Defence, told me: 'the best generals

Table 9.1 Dimensions of organizational cultures

Basic organization issues	Cultural responses
1 How emotionally bound up do people become with others in the work setting? (Affective orientation)	Unemotionality
2 How far do people attribute responsibility for personal problems to others, or to the system? (Animate–inanimate orientation to causality)	Depersonalization
3 How do people respond to differences in position, role, power and responsibility? (Hierarchical orientation)	Subordination
4 How far are people willing to embark with others on new ventures? (Change orientation)	Conservatism
5 How far do people choose to work alone or with and through others? (Individual–collectivist orientation)	Isolationism
6 How do people in different interest groups relate to each other? (Unitary–pluralistic orientation)	Antipathy

Source: Bate (1992: 232)

were the best trainers'. When I first arrived the President told me that he and his colleagues judged their own and others' performance by how people helped other people do well.

Third, the culture rewarded learning in a variety of ways. Because the culture was to me so distinctive it is worth describing fully.

In terms of Paul Bate's useful classification of dimensions of organizational cultures (Table 9.1) it is the total opposite of most UK organizations. The TPLF culture was highly emotional, highly personal, incredibly egalitarian, non-conservative, group-focused, constructive, integrative, and co-operative in its relations with others. It was evident that it placed value on intimacy, affection, closeness and fun. It stressed commitment, abhorred gossip, admired learning, openness and the process of review. It regarded rank as an indicator of level of commitment, sacrifice and contribution, not as an indicator of social distance, of differences in rewards, of status.

These qualities were interesting in themselves but their wider relevance lies in the question whether there was a relationship between these cultural values (according to Bate's classification) and the willingness to learn, to expose one's weaknesses and errors, to listen to and accept the good intentions of the criticisms of others. To put it starkly, are affection, egalitarianism and openness, necessary for learning to occur and for learning structures to work? Under what cultural conditions are we prepared to learn?

Fourth, members of the TPLF had very clear views about the importance and role of rewards and reward systems. They appreciated that behaviours advocated and required by the organization, and the strategy, must be rewarded culturally and by other means, and that these behaviours must be modelled by the senior members. They were clear that the rewards they mobilized – each others' respect, honour – were far more valuable than material, financial rewards. I heard of and saw numerous examples of these values. The most striking is the policy towards prisoners and defectors during the war. Government troops who were captured by or defected to the TPLF forces were allowed to choose from four options: they could return to their homes, which would mean that in due course they would be reconscripted and rejoin the fight against the TPLF; they could go to the liberated areas of Tigray and work; they could leave the country and go to the Sudan; or they could, if judged suitable, join the TPLF. I was told that the only crime for which the TPLF executed anyone was if TPLF fighters maltreated enemy prisoners. The policy of the government forces was to torture and execute captured TPLF fighters.

These responses to captured government troops were inspired by the values of the TPLF, who saw the conscripted government troops as victims of the Dergue's repressive policies. But it also contained a fascinating example of the strategic use of reward systems. What these policies actually achieved was the encouragement, on the part of government troops, of precisely the behaviour the TPLF wished to encourage. These policies encouraged government troops to desert, defect, surrender. Government troops returning to their army would quickly tell their colleagues how they had been treated; they would become propagandists for the TPLF within the Dergue forces. This would further weaken resolve, and encourage more troops to defect.

From our point of view the TPLF is a highly unusual organization. But the case of the TPLF may have some lessons for more conventional organizations in the West. For me this organization raised the following issues which seem to have a far wider application.

First, if learning is to be an organizational reality – a theory in use and not simply espoused – then learning has to be encouraged and facilitated through organizational structures, particularly structures of decision-making which encourage the flow of information and the ability of all levels and groups to know about and comment upon strategies and policies. To what extent do the structures of organizations that encourage learning differ from core structural values of most UK organizations. How often do we find such structure in existence? Are we prepared to advocate them? Are senior managers really prepared to sacrifice their 'rights' and decision-making habits and secrecy to achieve real learning structures?

Second, if learning can only occur when it is genuinely rewarded by the host organization, and when it is genuinely modelled and displayed by senior managers, then we need to consider how far conventional organizations do either of these things. What behaviours are really rewarded in most organizations? Do payment systems really *reward* learning (the supporting of others' performance), or do they reward the individual's own performance (which could be at the expense of others')? Do senior managers really *model* a willingness and capacity to learn? Do they reward those who help them learn? Think of how, if at all, senior managers manage their own learning. Think of their involvement in learning, or their role in others' learning. Do senior managers learn? Do they show that they learn, that they respect learning? How do senior managers support the learning of others?

Third, if learning needs certain sorts of cultural and relational support (intimacy, real trust and affection, lack of cliques and gossip) then how often do these exist, and what can be done to support their development? Are such cultural values possible in Western, individualistic, commercial organizations? What is our view of the relationship between the nature, quality, intensity of relationships and the possibility of learning, and how far are these relationship qualities achieved and achievable in organizations with which we work?

I was struck by Argyris's list of the norms supporting non-learning and how the TPLF way directly contradicted these practices on every count:

> Protect yourself unilaterally – by avoiding direct interpersonal confrontation and public discussion of sensitive issues that might expose you to blame;
>
> Protect others unilaterally by avoiding testing assumptions where the testing might evoke negative feelings and by keeping others from exposure to blame;
>
> Control the situation and the task – by making up your own mind about the problem and acting on your view, by keeping your view private and by avoiding the public enquiry which might refute your view.
>
> (Argyris, 1986: 40)

Fourth, are the conventional Western notions of leaders and the qualities on which leaders base their claims for legitimacy and respect, compatible with the encouragement of learning? Do leaders support egalitarianism, intimacy, and so on? Do they reflect respect for learning, for identifying and correcting performance? Are the best leaders the best learners and teachers in our experience? Is their emphasis on performance compatible with the need for learning to be based on processes? Can learning structures and cultures be compatible with hierarchical, highly stratified and inegalitarian organizations where leaders are remote and where leadership is defined in terms of being right, not of being willing to learn? One of the paradoxes I witnessed with the TPLF was the 'lack of respect' for the President: the teasing, the 'rudeness', the lack of decorum, the challenging on many real levels, allied to respect, but not a servile respect.

Senge supports this connection between cultures, learning and the role of leaders. He notes Schein's argument that 'most top executives are not qualified for the task of developing culture. Learning organisations represent a potentially significant evolution of organisational culture' (Senge, 1990: 22).

I was again struck by Argyris's remarks (1986) on the modelling significance of leaders. When talking about senior managers' behaviour he notes that subordinates learned to play it safe and take their cues from the behaviour of the executive. Since the subordinates sensed a gap or incongruence between the top people's behaviour and their stated values and policies, they tended to infer that it would embarrass them if they pointed out what seemed to them a discrepancy, and once the subordinates decided to follow this strategy they too were behaving in an incongruent manner.

Fifth, are relationships with key groups – workers, clients, suppliers, competitors, shareholders, banks, – defined and realized appropriately? Behind the rhetoric of every annual report, are these groups actually treated, actually involved, actually respected in the ways shown by the TPLF? Is there opposition where there could be co-operation? Are the 'right' behaviours defined and rewarded?

Sixth, given the TPLF's open, warm, supportive, honest and egalitarian culture, I wondered not only about the links between culture, structure and learning, but also about the sorts of culture regarded as normal in the UK – the contrast is striking. Where there was affection in TPLF, there is fear and anxiety in the UK. I was not sufficiently aware of how western organizations are characterized by loneliness, anxiety, distance, formality, and lack of trust.

Finally, this experience led me to revisit some of the classic texts on management and learning, and I was struck by the echoes and connections I found there. Argyris, for example, in his analysis of obstacles to learning notes the obstructive role of the

> disposition to treat interpersonal and intergroup conflict as undiscussable, the taboo on public analysis of corporate failures, the wish to avoid direct interpersonal confrontation – all these factors, and others related to them, contributed

both to the ineffectiveness of the corporation . . . and to the members' inability to diagnose and respond to patterns of ineffective development.

(Argyris and Schon, 1978: 43)

Few writers have been as perceptive as Argyris in detecting what goes wrong when learning does not occur. He maps the processes and stages of non-learning beautifully. But what his analysis possibly lacks is an understanding of the primary conditions underlying, and producing and supporting, learning and non-learning behaviours. The issue is not simply that we need to know what is involved in learning-focused activities, but that we need to identify what sorts of relationship are likely to produce and support these behaviours.

Similarly, I was struck by the perceptiveness of Argyris's insistence on the significance of the split between espoused theories and theories in use. He reports that his respondents in organizations which were dramatically poor at innovation,

spoke vividly, and with deep conviction about the import- ance of such factors as openness, risk-taking, internal commitment and the concern for truth. Time after time I was admonished about the importance of trusting the creative people and leaving them alone in their work . . . yet there may be an incongruence between what they say they value and how they behave. For example they tend to value directive leadership in getting a group to accomplish a task . . . Their openness and risk taking seem to be limited to those discussions and problems where emotions and inter- personal problems are not involved.

(Argyris, 1986: 194–5)

Achieving the 'learning organization' would thus necessitate structural and cultural change, often radical and uncomfortable. For example, the organizational culture must actually and genuinely promote and encourage learning – that is, people must be rewarded not just for achieving the obvious measures of performance, but also for their ability to help others. The culture would also have to encourage the practices and values which are necessary for learning – for example, openness, discussability, confrontation. Another thing would be for organizational structures and systems in themselves not to discourage learning, or its constituent elements and stages, but to facilitate it, for example, by facilitating open communication, discouraging deference, encouraging debate and discussion. Yet in most organizations employees have to find ways of overcoming the imposed structural boundaries in order to do what they believe they are there to do. Structures all too often obstruct the achievement of organizational objectives.

The question of what pro-learning organizational structures and cultures would be like is a very major issue in itself. The evidence is that such structures would have to overcome the notorious rigidities of traditional hierarchical bureaucracies and cultures, and would probably approximate more to the organic form described more than thirty years ago by Burns and Stalker (1961).

The organic type of organization – which is of course very similar indeed to the sort of organizational structure celebrated by Peters (1987) – would probably be more conducive to learning, for if it generates innovation it surely does this through encouraging learning, and if staff have to rely more on their own understanding of client or market needs, and less on compliance with rules, they must be learning. Also in this type of organization, knowledge and communication are located everywhere and flow freely.

For example, central to the Japanese organizational structure is the notion of *kaizen* – continuous improvement which results from particular organizational forms, principally team working with a core of flexible workers. However, although Japanese organizations may supply some answers to the question what structural forms encourage learning, they also teach a harsher lesson: that achieving a learning organization requires activity on a wide range of fronts, and that it demands serious, far-reaching (and probably uncomfortable) commitments and changes from senior managers not least to the very basis of the organization – the way the board define their role, and their relationship with the rest of the organization. The necessary structural changes are not only complex, but for most British companies they are probably very radical. They require major changes in structure, new work arrangements, a thorough break with traditional British elitism, genuine efforts to attract the commitment of the workforce, genuine reliance on worker initiative and creativity, with consequent reduction in managers' traditional conception of their 'right to manage' (which often means the right to make decisions in ways which are unaccountable and undiscussable). As long as the desire to become a learning organization remains at the level of exhortation, quality circles and team briefings (useful as these may be) and as long as residual patterns and structures of power, privilege and secrecy persist which reflect differences of interest and commitment between senior management and the rest of the organization, the learning organization will not often develop among large companies.

Some, of course, would prefer to define the concept in less structural terms, which are therefore more capable of being realized. It has been used in a rather minimal and restricted sense simply to describe a particular approach to training and development. This is the view of Barham *et al.* (1988), who use it to describe a situation where training and development are fundamental to the organization and are 'focused'.

Three key elements of this 'focused' approach are that: training and development and continuous learning by individuals are perceived as a necessity for organizational survival in a rapidly changing business environment; learning is linked to organizational strategy and to individual goals; and the emphasis is on on-the-job development, so that learning becomes a totally continuous activity (Barham *et al.*, 1988).

However, achieving a learning organization – in the more ambitious sense of Argyris and Senge – is obviously difficult and demanding. Many organizations aspire to such a goal, but few probably are fully prepared to adopt all the measures necessary to encourage and reward learning. Sadly, in many cases senior managers' references to the value of learning are probably more rhetorical than real. The culture in most organizations is probably anti-learning – because of the existence of rules and values and norms (probably all implicit and undiscussable) that encourage 'winning' over analysis and understanding, and encourage protection and defensiveness. Few organizations allow or encourage the values that Argyris and Schon identify with real learning: norms supporting valid information, free and informed choice and internal commitment.

However, if achieving structures and cultures that encourage learning of this type is difficult and ambitious, an alternative strategy is to focus not on structures, but on relationships; not on changing the organizational culture, but on changing the ways in which managers work with their staff. As Kolb *et al.* (1986: 14) have noted, the 'organisation's ability to survive and thrive in a complex dynamic environment is constrained by the capabilities of managers who must learn to manage both this greater environmental complexity and the complex organisational forms developed to cope with the environment'.

Probably the best and in most cases certainly the most feasible approach to achieving learning within organizations is to focus on the key role (that of manager) and the key process (the manager's concern and capacity to achieve the learning of subordinates). If managers see their individual responsibility in terms of the improvement of subordinates' work, if they are capable of managing this key role, and if they achieve it, many of the elements of the learning organization will be achieved. This view supports that of Mumford (1991: 24):

> We all know of individuals who manage to learn with little or no contribution from the organisation. It is however imposs-ible to conceive of a learning organisation without individual learners. The learning organisation depends absolutely on the skills, approaches, and commitment of individuals, to their own learning.

Regardless of how encouraging or discouraging the organiz-ational environment is to learning, it remains essential that individual managers recognize and implement their responsi-bility for the learning of their staff, and indeed of themselves. To quote Mumford again: 'It is crucial that we manage to improve the capacity of individuals to recognise and take advantage of learning opportunities, both those planned on a large scale and those which occur intimately on a smaller scale' (Mumford, 1991: 27). Even the individual manager working alone has a major opportunity to achieve a mini-learning organization within his or her sphere of influence and management. There is no need for managers to wait for the organization as a whole to become a learning organization before they work to achieve the learning of those around them. Even though organizational factors can certainly obstruct learning, these are not overwhelming in their impact. Indeed, probably the greatest single hindrance to the achievement of learning is managers' 'learned helplessness' – their conviction that nothing can be done until there is large-scale systematic change. This very attitude, of course, reproduces the obstacles themselves, while externalizing responsibility for managers' abdication from the key responsibilities of management.

But if managers are to define their role in terms of learning, and to accept this responsibility, it is also necessary to consider how managers can actually achieve this objective.

10

THE IMPORTANCE OF
MANAGEMENT STYLE

———

The achievement of performance improvement in others requires a number of prerequisites and skills of different types and at different levels; the rest of this book is concerned with identifying and discussing these prerequisites and skills. How can they be achieved? We have already identified four steps. The first is for managers to understand their role as already described; that is, to understand and accept that, despite the large number of things they do, the essentially managerial aspects of their role involves getting things done with and through other people.

The second step is to realize that if this responsibility is fundamental, then as managers they have major responsibility for, and commitment to, monitoring and improving the work of others (and of themselves).

This, in turn, requires consideration of the conditions under which adults learn, for improvement in performance is a form of learning.

It also requires that they understand and are able to achieve the appropriate form of relationship between themselves and others so that learning and performance improvement can occur. This issue now requires more focused attention.

Think, for example, of instances when people have tried to discuss your performance with you. Can you think of occasions when this was done well and badly? How did you feel on these occasions? How able or willing were you to change your behaviour as a result? Now think about the behaviour of the other people involved. What did they say and do? How would you characterize their attitude towards you on the basis of this?

Or think about occasions when you have tried to discuss performance issues with staff. How did you approach such discussions? What model did you hold in your head about the way people should behave when 'helping' others? How successful were you in putting this model into effect? It may help to think of extreme cases – disastrous occasions and successful ones. What did you do that contributed to the outcomes?

This issue is covered in the rest of this chapter. The analysis occurs in two main parts. To begin, we shall consider variations in management style and how these may impact on the capacity to address and resolve performance issues, particularly in relation to the practice of feedback as it is conventionally practised. Then we shall consider a framework for understanding the interplay between both parties to a potential delicate situation.

The issue here is *management style* , the way managers relate to others. Whether consciously or not, when managers relate to others, and particularly when they seek to discuss performance with them, they adopt one of a variety of management styles. What are the major types of approach used?

A useful distinction is between what Maier (1985) calls the 'tell', 'sell' and 'problem-solving' approaches. The first two are reasonably self-explanatory: telling involves informing the subordinate of what is wrong, and what should be done about it; selling involves the same elements but in a more persuasive manner. Problem-solving means approaching the issue of performance as a problem to be solved. Performance must presumably be a product of three elements: *specification* (is the subordinate clear about what is expected?); *capacity* (is the subordinate able to do what is required?); and *motivation* (is the person willing to do what is required?).

The problem-solving approach, which is recommended here, regards issues of performance as problems to be addressed mutually by both parties, with a view to uncovering which of these three elements is responsible for the problem. This approach also

LIVERPOOL JOHN MOORES UNIVERSITY
LEARNING SERVICES

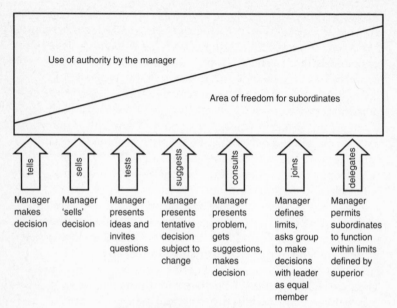

Figure 10.1 Management styles
Source: Tannenbaum and Schmidt (1958)

relies upon an understanding of how people learn, how they can be helped to learn, and upon the skills which this requires. It differs drastically from the tell and sell methods. These both assume that the manager uses authority vested in the role, simply to tell the subordinate the facts concerning what has happened and what is required in the way of solution or improved performance.

The problem-solving approach (which is often attractive to managers, indeed managers frequently seem to find great difficulty in not using it, for reasons which are discussed later) obviously takes managers' knowledge as given, so that their formal authority to impose a solution is backed up by their expertise and command of the facts on which the solution is based. This coincidence of rank and knowledge rarely occurs in reality. Ultimately, of course, the manager's solution can be enforced by the manipulation – or threat – of sanctions. As Argyris (1986) has noted, this approach springs from what is still probably a widely held but usually undiscussed and un-challenged management value: that work relationships are most effectively influenced through unilateral direction, coercion and control, and by by rewards and penalties that relate to these processes.

Figure 10.1, based on Tannenbaum and Schmidt's classification of types of management style, shows how these styles can vary from the hard 'tell' approach through suggestion to delegation. (It is important to realize that delegation is not abdication.) The 'tell' approach is located at the left-hand end of the continuum.

The use of any style probably varies with situation and with subordinate. But individuals also have personal preferences for particular management styles, based on personality, experience, views of management, etc. All too often individuals are not aware of how they manage, or of what it is like to be managed by them. Developing awareness of one's management style is a major step in initiating personal learning, and in learning about how you work with others to help (or hinder) their learning. What are the likely effects of an imposing, directing style on the achievement of the desired output, described above? Such a style is limited because managers provide instructions assuming they have complete data, and through experience and expertise can see the 'right' solution. This style will also be associated with close supervision and monitoring, so that senior managers can ensure that their solution is being implemented.

Would this approach produce the desired results as defined earlier – good-quality solutions to which all parties are committed and which enhance the working relationship? Almost certainly not. Though there may be some small role for this approach, particularly when there is no time for any other – as in a real crisis situation – it is unlikely to produce good-quality analyses and suggestions (for reasons which will be developed below) and will certainly not generate commitment. This is for three reasons.

First, it is empirically limited, with respect to its data. In its own highly limited terms it can only be valid when the manager has total knowledge, and when the solution does not need infor-mation from the other person, and when the manager knows exactly why performance is poor. Occasions of such managerial omniscience are rare. Of course managers may think they know

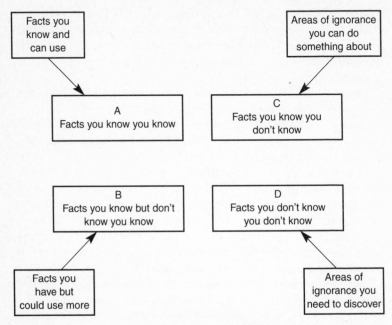

Figure 10.2 Knowing and not knowing
Source: Pedler *et al* (1986)

everything about the situation; not least because they 'know' the subordinate, or people of this type; or because from their experience they think they 'know' this sort of situation. Such common convictions are highly dangerous. They many be right some of the time; but sooner or later they will miss the mark; and what is worse, the manager will not know that s/he has missed the mark. I once offered to help a board of school governors by giving them some free instruction in interviewing techniques when they were about to interview to fill the post of head teacher. The chairman said that they were of course grateful but they felt they didn't need help in this area because they had had a lot of experience in recent years interviewing head teachers for this school. The models in their heads blocked them from realizing what they did not know, what they had not learnt.

Fundamental to the approach to managing performance advocated in this book is a crucial emphasis on managers questioning what they know, indeed, questioning whether they know, and thus approaching discussion of performance and performance improvement with an enquiring attitude. Within such discussions, identifying what needs to be known and who knows it is an important first step; behaving as if you did not know precisely when you are pretty sure that you do is crucial. Not knowing and knowing it is far less serious than not knowing that we do not know. Figure 10.2 is a useful charting of the possibilities of knowledge and ignorance. An important implication of this matrix is the need to move from C to A, D to B, and B to A in discussion, and the skills this will require.

Second, if success is measured partially in terms of achieving commitment to and involvement in a decision, then clearly this imposing, telling style will fail.

Problems of commitment are a product of the approach to problem-solving implicit in the assumption that problems are solved by one group or individual and then implemented by others. This distinction is absolutely fundamental to the structure of much management which involves the imposition (skilfully and persuasively) of 'elegant' (material) objectives on subordinates. Any system which separates design from implementation will encounter these problems, as will any analysis which distinguishes the values of design and commitment. Participation emerges from the way managers work with others; it is a product of a way of working, not a characteristic of an imposed managerial solution.

The 'telling' or imposing style of management will always systematically produce alienation among those to whom it is directed, in the same way as directive, deskilled approaches to shop-floor work create low-cost but poor-quality products. Such a reaction is no mere technical problem, but a direct result of the method. The approach, after all, does not allow subordinates actually to think or plan for themselves. The manager designs, the subordinates implement. It is managerial Taylorism, which aimed to achieve the separation, in work design, of design and execution, with design being vested in management. And like scientific management in the design of work it is unlikely to generate much commitment, and it is unlikely to prove an effective basis for organizational effectiveness. It will generate compliance, and it will produce obedience; but it will not attract creativity or require or develop intelligence.

Third, this approach to management is probably increasingly difficult to get away with, even if a manager chose to use it. The reason for this is that changes in organizations and in their environments make a firmly hierarchical style of management inappropriate. This is because of a change in power relations between managers and their subordinates. The importance of subordinates' involvement in organizational objectives, of their commitment to and responsibility for quality, of their crucial role in gathering and disseminating information, are all so well established that the disadvantages of a form of management which *imposed* solutions and information are extremely apparent and very generally accepted. As Mumford (1980: 10) remarks: 'at the moment managers are faced with recurrent problems of learning to manage in an environment where consent has to be sought and won'. Mumford identifies three key aspects of the changing environment which he sees as having significant impact on the ways managers need to work.

One impact is *complexity*, a major element of which is the growing importance of lateral rather than vertical organizational relationships. Sometimes this development is actually enshrined in changed organizational forms – for example, the matrix structure. Associated with the focus on lateral relationships is an emphasis on influence based not on position but on knowledge, competence and information. Again this undermines a hierarchically dominated management style.

Second, Mumford points to the increase in *management conflict* occasioned by dual reporting roles and structurally based ambiguity. 'Conflict' may be too strong a word: what is at issue here, however, is that these changes may require managers to make choices between priorities and demands.

Third, and this may not be a new factor but a consequence of the earlier two, managers are increasingly faced with what Mumford calls a *paradox*: managers need to clarify issues of priorities and ambiguity, but this clarification actually reveals the 'fact and necessity of interdependence . . . requiring a sharing of information and commitment at some level to a consensus on what should be done. Ambiguity of objectives is replaced by ambiguity of authority' (Mumford, 1980: 12). In other words the process of clarification reveals inherent ambiguity. These developments put further pressure on the development of a mode of managing which does not rely on the simple and straightforward exercise of formalized organizational authority.

If we want commitment and superior solutions we have to think of another way of managing. There are two possibilities on offer. The first, which is a product of the styles of management described in the middle of Figure 10.2, involves the skilful use of persuasion, selling and manipulation to win at least acceptance of the manager's solution and point of view. It is very common, particularly in selling and broking cultures. It can seem to work, but it really does not. Strangely, managers who use this approach often insist that it works and that subordinates really are persuaded of the merits of the manager's point of view and accept it as their own. But if you ask these same managers if they notice when their manager tries to sell to them, they claim they can spot it immediately. It is hard to believe that their subordinates are not similarly aware of what is being done to them.

This approach is not advocated here, despite its apparent appeal: ultimately, although it may appear to generate support, it does not develop real commitment; nor does it generate good-quality solutions, data and analysis, for the traffic is still largely, if not entirely, one-way. Thus although the style may be charming and winning, the content does not really differ significantly from the 'tell' method, except in the charm factor.

The second way to achieve commitment is in fact the only way: through genuine involvement – the 'problem-solving' approach. People will be committed to processes and outcomes to which they have contributed and in which they have been involved. Thus it is necessary to encourage and allow collective and open participation and involvement in the process of discussion. Note that this does not mean that managers hand over to subordinates; they simply share responsibility and participation. Thus actual commitment can only be achieved through real participation and involvement.

Fletcher (1986) has noted a number of studies of appraisal systems which report that managers avoided appraisal because they disliked judging their colleagues and staff. He reports a study by Meyer which found 'that appraisal interviews which sought both to give feedback and produce an increase in subordinate motivation (and thus in performance) tended to reduce motivation and brought little or no change in behaviour' (Fletcher 1986:4). Meyer and Fletcher recommend a type of appraisal (or performance review) where there are more frequent discussions of performance with no judgements or ratings made, which did not discuss salary and where the emphasis was on participative goal-setting and problem-solving.

So we arrive at the conclusion that the desired type of output as described above (good-quality solutions, commitment, learning) is only likely to be achieved through interactions between managers and their subordinates which are two-way, genuinely open to contributions from all sides, not 'telling'-focused: the quality of solutions and suggestions is dependent upon the open processes of discussion and analysis in which both boss and subordinates are involved, and which produce commitment. This way you achieve both good-quality solutions and commitment to these solutions at one and the same time. This is the way to achieve the key outcomes of learning as defined earlier by Argyris: valid information (data), free and informed choice analysis of implications, costs, reasons and internal commitment. And as Kanter (1989a: 91–2) remarks:

> The chance to learn new skills or apply them in new arenas is an important motivator in a turbulent environment because it's oriented towards securing the future. 'The learning organization' promises to become a 1990s business buzzword as companies seek to learn more systematically from their experiences and to encourage learning from their people. In the world of high technology, where people understand uncertainty, the attractiveness of any company often lies in its capacity to provide learning and experience. By this calculus, access to training, mentors, and challenging projects is more important than pay or benefits.

We are claiming that these benefits must not be restricted to high-technology organizations only: they are important generally.

We now need to explore the processes, content and stages of these quintessential managerial situations.

Feedback

It is useful to distinguish between the approach advocated here and that technique commonly known as *feedback*. Feedback refers to the information we receive after we have done something. Performance improvement is not possible without it. If we do not know how we have done we don't know that we need to do things differently. Management textbooks and management courses place great emphasis on feedback, and on managers' responsibilities for generating feedback for their subordinates. But we need to look more closely at the implications of the expression 'feedback' for the source of performance data, the way it is delivered and, crucially, its impact. It is worth spending some time on this, not only because the feedback model is so prevalent that it may well be regarded as *the* major or indeed the only way to assist others' learning, but also because by analysing the feedback model our own model may, in contrast, begin to become clearer.

The application of the expression 'feedback' in organizational settings is metaphorical, deriving from its occurrence in systems, particularly mechanical and electrical systems. The use of the expression with reference to the management of performance improvement argues essentially and implicitly that the operation of feedback within systems is similar or analogous to the operation of human learning and improvement within organizations. Within systems feedback operates simply (however complex the technology): information on the key system property is measured, and at certain levels, is fed back to the system and affects it as a whole or the operation of some aspect of it – closing it down or starting it up, slowing it or quickening it. A familiar example would be the role of the thermostat in heating or cooling systems. When the temperature, as measured by the thermostat, reaches a certain set level, information is fed back to another part of the system to start or to close boilers or fans which will restore the system to equilibrium.

Now the danger with using a metaphor is that we forget its origins, and overlook its limitations. In a very, very simple way you could say that the achievement of human learning is *like* a feedback loop: behaviour produces certain consequences; these are brought to our attention; we change our behaviour to remove undesirable effects or to produce desirable ones.

But there are also very serious difficulties with the model, which limit the efficiency of conventional models of feedback in management when seen as a model of learning, for attempts to address performance issues and to achieve improvements which are based on the feedback model do in fact proceed as if individual managers were broadly similar to central heating boilers. But they are not, and they learn in different ways.

There are certain aspects of the feedback model of learning which are inappropriate for human learning. First, within mechanical and electronic systems, feedback information is always accurate, appropriate and undeniable: thermometers do not make mistakes about temperature levels. But human performance data are not always accurate (indeed, are probably never entirely accurate), and people often make mistakes about performance data.

Second, the origin of feedback data is irrelevant: the boiler does not care where the signals are coming from. The origin of human performance data is not irrelevant to the receiver.

Third, the instruction inherent in feedback data is always correct, and the system is perfectly able to respond to it. Neither of these conditions is true in human learning.

Fourth, the mechanical or electronic system which receives feedback data has no feelings about the information (commitment is not an issue with central heating boilers); it is fully able to respond appropriately. Central heating boilers are not instructed by the thermostat to do things beyond their capacity; and have no choice (motivation is not a problem either). None of these conditions applies to human learning.

Fifth, the communication of feedback information requires no skill, poses no risks to the relationship between the two systems concerned, cannot go wrong, or produce inappropriate or counter-productive consequences. None of these is true of human learning situations, where all these things are only too likely. To support learning in others, to assist the identification of difficulties and consequences and the recognition of good-quality solutions requires considerable skill. Clearly the key skills are communication skills; and equally clearly they will centre around the use of communication categories or behaviour, which elicit information, which seek data and encourage analysis, rather than communication behaviours which impose solutions, inform and instruct. There is research evidence to support our recommendation that the most relevant communication categories are those that involve seeking data and ideas.

The model of feedback or learning applicable to human situations is therefore very different indeed from mechanical feedback processes – more complex, uncertain and vulnerable, and requiring far more skill and understanding.

Achieving improvement in people's performance can only be done through the people concerned – with their involvement. Good-quality solutions require information, ideas, analysis and suggestions from both parties; they also require the commitment of both parties, and this is crucial to the development of the necessary motivation. And as Mumford (1980: 70) notes:

> For many managers, motivation is something which you pump into others. . . . Motivation is in fact something intrinsic to a person, not the result of someone else's manipulation. Intrinsic motivation can be encouraged or discouraged, but a manager cannot be motivated to learn by someone else or by some external event: these can only release a motivation to learn which the manager already has.

It follows that the management of improvement involves, as a central element, the structuring and managing of a process whereby both parties address issues of performance, think about it and agree solutions which are likely to produce improvement, and thus liberate an inherent motivation within the manager. (The source and nature of this motivation need not detain us, unless it were to be seriously argued that managers have *no* inherent interest in improving the quality of their work.)

Transactional analysis and adult–adult relationships

But what if the 'other' in the relationship does not see the relationship in the same way? What if the 'other', for whatever reason, wishes not to be involved in a process which will lead him or her to take responsibility for personal improvement? How can we understand such a situation and work to correct it? Of value here is a model of how people interact when they communicate with each other. It is called *transactional analysis* (TA), and was originally developed by Eric Berne. It helps explain why communications go wrong; and offers some suggestions for ways out of communications problems.

TA argues that each individual is a complex and shifting combination of three distinct conditions which Berne calls *ego-states*. At any time one is dominant, and will influence the way the individual reacts or behaves. Since each ego-state is associated with very different sorts of behaviour, it helps us to know which ego-state we, or others, are in.

The first ego-state we consider is the *parent* state. As the name suggests, it is associated with typical parental behaviour, which individuals may well pick up from their parents. It is associated with authority, judgement, prescription, morality and guilt. Berne distinguishes two aspects of the parent state. One of these is the *critical parent*. This ego-state is characterized by authority and prescription. It is largely one-way. Non-verbally, it is indicated by frowning, accusing, pointing and finger-wagging. The other aspect is the *nurturing parent*, characterized by sympathy, protectiveness and cosseting. The nurturing parent knows best, and knows that the child is not yet ready, but needs help and guidance.

Both these parent states have a role; but clearly both have negative implications when used excessively within a performance-improvement context. Both stifle learning, albeit from different positions. Neither encourages the other person to think about and take responsibility for, his or her development or learning.

The second ego-state is the *adult* state. This is concerned with rationality, objectivity and facts. It is unemotional, detached. The non-verbal behaviour is calm, level-toned, thoughtful, enquiring and balanced.

The third ego-state is the *child* state. Berne distinguishes three types of child. The *free child* is natural, spontaneous, fun-loving, creative, uninhibited. The *adapted child* displays the more devious behaviour that we have learnt gets us recognition and reward. It involves flattery, dissimulation, dissembling and deviousness; the adapted child is compliant, dejected, sulking. The third type of child is the *little professor* – this is evident when thinking is used manipulatively, to score points or to undermine.

There are two major implications of this model. First, it means that at any time each one of us is predominantly in a particular ego-state (sometimes we move very quickly from one to the other). And our behaviour will be very different, depending on which state we are in. For example, think back to an occasion where you were discussing your work performance with some-one. Try to recall what state you were in, and how this influenced your approach and your reactions.

Second, it is useful, when an interaction is important, to be aware (at least at some level) of what state we are in, and, crucially, what state the other is in. Imagine, for example, that we want to have a discussion about performance and the other person insists: 'It wasn't my fault. I know it went wrong, I just don't seem to be able to do it, I don't know why.' This suggests a child state response. This is not appropriate for a calm and reasoned discussion of performance. Therefore it becomes necessary to try to move the other person into the adult state. The principal way in which this is done is first not to accept the implicit invitation to respond to the other's child or parent state by moving into the related state (child to parent, parent to child); and second, by using the classic adult responses of open questions, responding with calm curiosity and interest to the other's responses, claims and denials.

The third implication of the TA model is that ego-states tend to respond to each other. The parent, as initiator, tends to 'hook' the child in the other person, and vice versa. So a highly censorious, prescriptive manager telling off the subordinate, and telling him how the job should have been done, is likely to produce a response of avoidance, defensiveness, or pathetic dependence – all child reactions. The problem with this is that neither party will learn, the outcome of the discussion will be poor and ill based and the receiving party will not be committed – the ideas will be the boss's ideas. If they fail – and they probably will – it is the boss's fault.

The TA model is particularly useful within a management context, and it is particularly pertinent when managers are addressing issues of performance and seeking to achieve improvement, for in these discussions it is critical that the participants achieve an adult–adult relationship, yet the temptation, if either the 'tell' or 'sell' approach is used, is for managers to slip into the critical parent role, and thus to produce the child in the other, who avoids the point, refuses to take responsibility, seeks to confuse the issue, makes unreasonable demands, blames others and plays games. This will not produce learning.

In Chapter 11, you will be asked to observe a manager–subordinate interaction and to try to identify the ego-states the participants are in at various phases, if they change, when they change state, and what is said or done to bring about a change of state or to maintain adult–adult interaction.

Learning skills

The approach to key management skills relevant to the achievement of learning is supported by the MCI charter approach and by Boyatzis. The MCI identifies four key managerial roles. Three are technical: managing finance; managing information; and managing operations. It is true, of course, that managers frequently have to do some or all of these things; but we do not see them as managerial in essence, as explained earlier. Management in our sense is the fourth of the MCI competences: managing people. This role includes three components which are directly pertinent to the approach here: develop team, individuals and self to enhance performance; plan, allocate and evaluate work carried out by team, individual and self; and create, maintain and enhance effective working relationships.

Boyatzis's list of management competences, listed earlier in Table 4.3 is also seen as broadly concerned with, or relevant to, the management of others.

Furthermore, the MCI offers some sensible and useful guidelines. The three clusters, 'Planning to optimise achievement of results', 'Managing others to optimise results', and 'Using intellect to optimise results', certainly map the general terrain covered here and describe the intentions of the learning process. But they do not go far enough. They may pretty well describe what managers should do. But they do not explain *how* managers should perform these activities successfully nor, crucially, do they address why managers may find this difficult. The MCI competences do focus on the same key requirements and skills, but we must consider what managers have to do – and to avoid doing – in order to achieve these goals. We need to consider the behaviours necessary to achieve these objectives, specifically the language behaviours, for learning is achieved through language.

Mumford offers some useful suggestions for the behaviours of good developers. The list is worth quoting in full because it anticipates in some detail the later discussion of key behaviours. Mumford (1980: 4) notes that bosses who are good conscious developers of their subordinates have the following characteristics:

- They draw out the strengths and weaknesses of their subordinates, rather than suppressing them.
- They reward their people both materially and psychologically for the risks they take in attempting to develop themselves.
- They positively seek to identify learning opportunities for their subordinates.
- They give personal time to the development of subordinates – for example in reviewing and analysing an activity for learning purposes.
- They involve their subordinates in some of their own important tasks (not just delegate Mickey Mouse tasks).
- They share some of their problems and anxieties with their subordinates, and in the interest of their subordinates' development rather than simply as relief for themselves.
- They listen rather than talk.
- They do not say or imply 'be more like me'.
- They take risks on the desired results of their unit in pursuit of relevant learning opportunities for their people.

But, Mumford (1980: 4), adds 'there are very few managers who are prepared to behave in this way'. He attributes this to aspects of organizational (see Chapter 8) and to the psychological make-up of the managers. We would prefer to see this as a case of skilled incompetence – see the discussion below. Another major reason is a lack of understanding of the need to do these things – that management involves, centrally, this responsibility for others' performance. There is also a difficulty that managers do not know how to do the things in the list – how to *craft* language to achieve these desirable but elusive features.

Kolb *et al.* (1986) also contribute to this discussion of the skills managers need to manage learning. Recognizing that organizations have moved or are moving away from the classical organization, with its limited span of control, non-overlapping job definitions, a single chain of command and formal authority matching responsibility, these authors, building on the four stages of the learning cycle, identify four core competences:

> Greater behavioural competence in taking initiative and responsibility under conditions of risk and uncertainty, greater perceptual competence in gathering and organising information and taking the perspective of different organisational sub-units, greater affective competence in empathising with others and resolving conflicts among managers with different viewpoints and greater symbolic competence in one's ability to conceptualise the organisational as a system are required to to make modern organisational forms work effectively.
>
> (Kolb *et al.*, 1986: 15)

The interesting thing about this list (apart from its echoes of some of the points made earlier in the discussion of the TPLF as a learning organization – note the value placed on affective competence . . .) is the connections the authors make between these competences and the stages of the learning cycle. The four competences are basically the skills of using the learning cycle with others – exactly the skills of managing learning that this book has advocated:

> affective competences (e.g. being sensitive to people's feelings) are related to the concrete experiences mode; perceptual competences (e.g. gathering information) are related to the reflective observation mode; symbolic competences (e.g. building conceptual models) are related to the abstract

conceptualisation mode; and behavioural competences (e.g. making decisions) are related to the active experimentation learning mode.

(Kolb *et al.*, 1986: 16)

The language of learning

From earlier discussions it is clear that crafting appropriate language within learning-focused discussions is absolutely critical. What managers do when they work with others to improve what they do and how they do it, is talk and listen. How they do these things, and the proportion of time they spend on each, will seriously affect how effectively they help others learn. It will also be clear that many managers find the achievement of the appropriate types of language difficult.

If you think back to the discussion of management style, the discussion of TA, and the discussion of the learning styles, you will have noted that, in every case, it was suggested that achieving the appropriate (problem-solving) management styles, achieving adult–adult relationships, and supporting colleagues around the four stages of the learning cycle, required distinctive forms of language. Are there distinctive and identifiable types of language that are associated with successful and unsuccessful attempts to encourage and support someone's learning?

Figure 10.3 offers a useful classification of the sorts of language managers use when discussing performance. Crudely, it is possible to distinguish 'push' from 'pull' types of language. 'Push' is when the speaker informs, instructs, criticizes and gives or imposes assessments, suggestions and evaluations. 'Pull' is when the language used seeks to elicit ideas, suggestions, reactions or feelings.

Managers who are more successful in supporting the learning of their colleagues will engage in more *pull* types of language than *push* types. By 'pull' we mean seeking information, testing information, and building. These are the sorts of language category people use when they try to investigate, to find out. 'Push' types of language mean proposing, giving information

	Date: 24.2.71	Group: C			Date: SBT	Group: 14		
Name	Jean	Mike	John	Mark	Peter	Jim		TOTAL
Supporting	HHT III	HHT HHT HHT II	II	IIII	IIII	HHT		
Disagreeing		HHT III	II	I	I	IIII		
Building		HHT III	III	IIII	IIII	HHT I		
Criticizing		II			II	I		
Bringing in	IIII	HHT III				HHT		
Shutting out	II	IIII	II	III	II	II		
Innovating		III				II		
Solidifying	III	II	I	III		HHT I		
Admitting difficulty		II	I			I		
Defending/attacking		II						
Giving information	HHT HHT II	HHT HHT HHT HHT HHT HHT I	HHT HHT HHT II	HHT HHT IIII	HHT HHT HHT III	HHT HHT HHT HHT HHT HHT I		
Seeking information	HHT II	HHT HHT HHT HHT HHT HHT I	I	HHT HHT I	II	HHT II		
Other								

Figure 10.3 Communication categories
Source: Rackham *et al*. (1971)

and shutting out. We use these because we wish to tell, because we think we know already.

'Seeking information' covers a multitude of ways in which information, suggestions, proposals, etc. are *elicited* from the other. This category includes questioning, and the ways in which managers question can be an important source of ineffectiveness. All too often managers ask closed and leading questions in which, thinly disguised, they offer their views, assumptions and beliefs to others for them to agree or disagree. Yet they may not realize that they are doing this: they may think that they are actually asking open and non-directive questions.

How can we explain that managers who genuinely wish to generate learning in others (even themselves) can use language which obstructs this objective; and that they fail to notice (and hence correct) their responsibility for the failure of their efforts? (In fact the situation is probably even worse than this: when they fail to assist learning they may attribute the failure to the other person.)

We explain this mismatch between intention and effect in terms of a specific and pervasive skill called *linguistic incompetence*. If managers use ineffective, incompetent types of language this is not because they are simply incompetent; on the contrary, it is because they are competent, in fact highly skilled, at acting in unhelpful ways. There are two aspects of this: the use of 'push' instead of 'pull' categories; and the use, even while 'seeking information' of closed forms of questioning.

Test this for yourself. Next time you hear people (or indeed yourself) seeking information from others, observe and list the questions that are used and try to categorize them in terms of open and closed question types. Open questions are those that make no attempt to impose or restrict an answer. Closed questions can be answered with a yes or no; or questions that simply offer a choice of alternatives. They actually tell the person being questioned what the questioner expects or wants to hear.

If managers tend to used closed questions, why is this? Why is it that managers are so drawn to 'push' categories that even when trying to elicit information they formulate questions in such a closed manner that they actually gain very little information – or indeed information that is hopelessly contaminated by their questions? How can people behave incompetently when they are trying to be competent? How can they behave incompetently with such skill? The answer must lie in some basic confusion about the nature of competence and about how you behave when you are being competent. Could it be that managers use 'push' – in this context incompetent – type language precisely because somehow they have learnt to see this as being competent?

To clarify this issue we need to go back to the discussion early in this book of the management role. There we noted that managers typically fill a variety of roles, out of which we distinguished and focused on, the essentially managerial aspect, and chose to ignore the technical, business and other aspects. But if we, for our present purposes, can ignore these aspects of the manager's role, managers themselves may find this distinction less easy. For the other roles managers fill have implications for how they fill the managerial element.

If managers, through their training and development, learn to overuse the 'push' and to underuse the 'pull' types of language – to tell too much and to ask too little – this may be because they have learnt to define – and been rewarded for defining – competence, and confidence in their competence, in terms of telling. For their very achievement of management positions is based on their successful performance of non-managerial technical functions – and incumbency of these roles requires and demands knowledge, expertise, certainty and conviction.

As technical specialists and experts, in whatever function, managers must master knowledge and techniques, on the basis of which they make authoritative decisions, give authoritative advice, know what they're doing. Competent people have the answers. For many managers being exposed as not knowing what they are doing, or not knowing what is going on, is the worst thing that can happen. In these roles managers see themselves as being as good as they are knowledgeable – they are as competent as they are right. If this is true it has devastating consequences for managers' language behaviour. If being knowledgeable, fully informed, expertly qualified, are the bases of recognized competence, then these conditions will result, understandably and obviously, in managers defining competence in terms of knowing the answers, being in command, and thus in terms of using this knowledge mastery to hand down prescriptive information and to evaluate others. All these lead, naturally to 'telling' forms of language behaviour, and equally naturally lead away from questioning forms. For this is how you display knowledge and mastery.

In these circumstances asking questions, particularly open questions, is seen as indicating not just curiosity, but, much worse, *ignorance*. And if competent managers *know* the answers, asking open questions which carry no implication of the expected or desired answer, suggests you do not know; therefore, in terms of dominant conceptions of performance, that you are incompetent. Otherwise you wouldn't have to ask. The idea that questions might help someone else learn is not only foreign, not only an indication of incompetence, it is probably not seen as a necessary aspect of the job. The job is to make sure that *you* know; others' knowledge or ignorance is their problem.

According to this view, therefore, if you have to frame a question, design it so that it shows that you know already. Use the question to do two things: ostensibly to gain information and to show interest, but, much more importantly, to show that as a competent manager you know the answer already, or, on the basis of much experience and wisdom, that you can imagine the answer.

It is here that managers' difficulties with genuinely eliciting with using open questioning lie. The problem is simply a technical one. Managers find open questioning and other 'pull' types of language hard because to be competent (open) questioners, they have to risk their own competence, as they see it. Thus to be able to help others learn they not only have to learn the matters covered in this book, but, more fundamentally, they have to unlearn what they have already learned and to learn to behave as if they were ignorant. And they may learn that they were. When managers behave as if they did not know – by asking open, probing questions – they will begin to learn; possibly to learn that they did not know. If they insist on behaving as if they know already they will not learn that they did not know. But most of all, they must learn that only by behaving 'incompetently' in terms of their previous conceptions of competence, can they master the most fundamental of all managerial competences: that of behaving as if they do not know, in order to help themselves and others learn.

133

11

IMPROVING THE
MANAGEMENT OF LEARNING

In this final chapter you are encouraged to apply the ideas, frameworks, and models discussed in this book to actual examples of management work. It is suggested that you observe and analyse actual discussions between managers and their subordinates aimed at improving performance (or finding out and sorting out what went wrong, or reviewing an item of work, etc.). Your objective is to practise analysing these discussions in terms of the ideas contained in this book, and recognizing what the key ideas of the book mean and look like in practice. The intention is to help you make the transition from your reading and understanding of the text to your independent ability to recognize and apply these materials to examples of actual managerial work.

Further than this, by viewing and reviewing the examples of managerial work you will begin to develop some techniques and ideas for handling such conversations yourself. This framework can be used as a basis for your own skill development.

When considering your cases, you are asked to look out for the following:

1 What conception of 'appropriate' *management style* do the managers use during the discussion, and what management style do they seem to wish to achieve, when talking about their

objectives and strategy before the discussion? What evidence from the discussions would you use to support your views? What are the consequences of the management style they use for the progress (or lack of progress) of the discussion, and for the achievement (or non-achievement) of the objectives? What facilitates or obstructs the achievement of an appropriate form of management style? How does it (if it is single and unitary) contribute to the outcome of the discussion?

2 How would you characterize the *relationship* between the participants in terms of the transactional analysis categories? How does the relationship vary over the course of the discussion? What sort of relationship did the managers wish to achieve, from their pre-discussion remarks? (Even though they are unlikely to use the language of TA, it is still possible to get a pretty good general idea of what sort of relationship they wished to achieve.) What sort of relationship was actually achieved?

How is the particular style of relationship achieved? In particular, try to identify the different types of language strategy and behaviour which are associated with different TA styles: that is, once you have identified each 'position' or ego-state, list the forms of language associated with these. It is especially important to identify the forms of language used to achieve and maintain the adult ego-state. Achieving an adult–adult relationship in the sort of delicate discussions of performance which often take place can be very difficult. The person whose performance is under analysis may be tempted into a child-ego state. This can easily 'hook' the parent in the other participant. Look out for this. Similarly, getting someone who is in the child state to move to the adult requires skill and perseverance. Can you find occasions where managers successfully persuade the other person to move from child to adult? How do they do it?

3 How do managers seek to *achieve learning* with subordinates? Do the managers seem to have (or to claim) a strategy for achieving performance improvement? How, if at all, might it relate to the learning cycle described earlier? If there is a learning strategy and if it does approximate to the learning cycle, then how does the strategy relate to the model of learning? Specifically, which stages of the learning cycle are covered in the discussion?

4 What *language skills* are used? There is great advantage in understanding the role of language skills in the management of improvement, and being able to identify the key communication skills. You are encouraged to look out for and take note of the sorts of language category that are used in the performance-management discussions that take place around you – or indeed in your own discussions. Use the classification of communication categories listed earlier, in Figure 10.3. Being aware of the language people use in these discussions, and being aware of the consequences of the language used for the achievement of the objectives of the discussion is a crucial first step in developing one's own skills.

REFERENCES

Argyris, C. (1970) *Intervention Theory and Method*. Reading, Mass.: Addison-Wesley.

Argyris, C. (1986) *Change and Defensive Routines*. Boston, Mass.: Pitman.

Argyris, C. (1990) *Overcoming Organisational Defenses*. London: Allyn and Bacon.

Argyris, C. (1992) A leadership dilemma: Skilled incompetence, in G. Salaman, S. Cameron, H. Hamblin, P. Iles, C. Maybe and K. Thompson (eds) *Human Resource Strategies*. London: Sage, 82–94.

Argyris, C. and Schon, D. (1978) *Organisational Learning: A Theory of Action Perspective*. Reading, Mass.: Addison-Wesley.

Barham, K., Fraser, J. and Heath L. (1988) *Management For the Future*. Berkhampstead: Ashridge Management College and Foundation for Management Education.

Bate, P. (1992) The impact of organisational culture on approaches to organisational problem solving, in G. Salaman, S. Cameron, H. Hamblin, P. Iles, C. Maybe and K. Thompson (eds) *Human Resource Strategies*. London: Sage, 213–36.

Beaumont, P. (1993) *Human Resource Management : Key Concepts and Skills*. London: Sage.

Beer, M. and Spector, B. (eds) (1985) *Readings in Human Resources Management*. New York: Free Press.

Beer, M., Spector, B., Lawrence, P.R., Mills, Q.N. and Walton, R.E. (1984) *Managing Human Assets*. New York: Free Press.

Beer, M., Spector, B., Lawrence, P., Mills, Q.N. and Walton, R.E. (1985)

Human Resource Management: A General Manager's Perspective. New York: Free Press.

Beer, M., Eisenstadt, R. and Spector, B. (1988) *The Critical Path to Change: Developing the Competitive Organisation*. Boston, Mass.: Harvard Business School Press.

Beer, M., Eisenstadt, R. and Spector, B. (1990) Why change programs don't produce change. *Harvard Business Review*, November–December, 158–66.

Bendix, R. (1956) *Work and Authority in Industry*. New York: Harper.

Blyton, P. and Turnbull, P. (1992) HRM: Debates, dilemmas and contradictions, in P. Blyton and P. Turnbull (eds) *Reassessing Human Resource Management*. London: Sage, 260–72.

Boam, R. and Sparrow, P. (1992) The rise and rationale of competency-based approaches, in R. Boam and P. Sparrow (eds) *Designing and Achieving Competency*. Maidenhead: McGraw-Hill, 3–15.

Boyatzis, R.E. (1982) *The Competent Manager*. Chichester: John Wiley.

Boyatzis, R.E. (1992) Building on competence: The effective use of managerial talent, in G. Salaman, S. Cameron, H. Hamblin, P. Iles, C. Maybe and K. Thompson (eds) *Human Resource Strategies*. London: Sage.

Burgoyne, J.G. and Hodgson, V.E. (1983) Natural learning and managerial action. *Journal of Management Studies*, 20(3), 387–99.

Burns, T. and Stalker, G.M. (1961) *The Management of Innovation*. London: Tavistock.

Carlson, S. (1951) *Executive Behaviour*. Stockholm: Strombergs.

Champy, J. (1994) Time to re-engineer the manager. *Financial Times*, 14 January.

Cockerill, T. (1989) The kind of competence for rapid change. *Personnel Management*, 21(9), 52–6.

Constable, J. and McCormick, R. (1987) *The Making of British Managers*. London: BIM and CBI.

Cressey, J. and Jones, B. (1992) Business strategy and the human resource: Last links in the chain?, in *Human Resource Strategies, Supplementary Readings, 1*. Milton Keynes: Open University, 61–74.

Dalton, M. (1959) *Men Who Manage*. New York: McGraw-Hill.

Dertouzos, M., Lester, R. and Solow, R. (1989) *Made in America: Regaining the Competitive Edge*. Cambridge, Mass.: MIT Press.

Drucker, P. (1988) Management and the world's work. *Harvard Business Review*, September–October, 75–6.

Fletcher, C. (1986) Effects of performance review in appraisal: Evidence and implications. *Journal of Management Development*, 5(3), 3–12.

Fletcher, S. (1992) *Competence-Based Assessment Techniques*. London: Kogan Page.

References

Fombrun, C.J. and Tichy, N.M. (1983) Strategic planning and human resources management: At rainbow's end, in R. Lamb (ed.) *Recent Advances in Strategic Planning*. New York: McGraw-Hill.

Fombrun, C.J., Tichy, N.M. and Devanna, M.A. (1984) *Strategic Human Resource Management*. New York: John Wiley.

Guest, D. (1987) Human resource management and industrial relations. *Journal of Management Studies*, 24(5), 503–22.

Hales, C.P. (1986) What do managers do? *Journal of Management Studies*, 23, 88–115.

Handy, C. (1987) *The Making of British Managers*. London: NEDO.

Hendry, C. and Pettigrew, A. (1986) The practice of strategic human resource management. *Personnel Review*, 15(5), 3–8.

Hendry, C. and Pettigrew, A. (1990) Human resource management: An agenda for the 1990s. *International Journal of Human Resource Management*, 1(1), 17–43.

Honey, P. and Mumford, A. (1986) *The Manual of Learning Styles*. Maidenhead: Honey.

Iles, P. (1992) Managing assessment and selection processes, Unit 8. *Human Resource Strategies*. Milton Keynes: Open University.

Jacobs, R. (1989) Getting the measure of management competence. *Personnel Management*, 21(6) 32b–37.

Janis, I. (1982) *Victims of Groupthink*. Boston, Mass.: Houghton-Mifflin.

Kanter, R. (1989a) *When Giants Learn to Dance*. London: Unwin-Hyman.

Kanter, R. (1989b) The new managerial work. *Harvard Business Review*, November–December, 80–92.

Klemp, G.O. (1980) *The Assessment of Occupational Competence*. Report to the National Institute of Education, Washington DC.

Kolb, D.A. (1984) *Experimental Learning: Experience as the Source of Learning and Development*. Englewood Cliffs, N.J.: Prentice-Hall.

Kolb, D. and Fry, R. (1975) Towards an applied theory of experimental learning, in C.L. Cooper (ed.) *Theories of Group Processes*. Chichester: John Wiley, 33–57.

Kolb, D., Rubin, I. and McIntyre, J. (1984) *Organisational Psychology: An Experimental Approach to Organisational Behaviour*. Englewood Cliffs, N.J.: Prentice-Hall.

Kolb, D., Lublin, S., Spoth, J. and Baker, R. (1986) Strategic management development. *Journal of Management Development*, 5(3), 13–24.

Kotter, J. (1982) *The General Manager*. New York: Free Press.

Luthans, F., Rosenkratz, S. and Hennessey, H. (1985) What do successful managers really do? *Journal of Applied Behavioural Science*, 21(3), 255–70.

Maier, N.R.F. (1985) Three types of appraisal interview. *Personnel*, March–April, 27–40.

Management Charter Initiative (MCI) (1991) *Management Standards Implementation Pack*. London: MCI.

Mangham, I. and Silver, M. (1987) *Management Training, Context and Practice*. London: ESRC Pilot Survey on Management Training.

Martinko, M. and Gardner, W. (1990) Structured observation of managerial work. *Journal of Management Studies*, 27(3), 329–55.

Mintzberg, H. (1980) *The Nature of Managerial Work*. Englewood Cliffs, N.J.: Prentice-Hall.

Mintzberg, H. (1990) The manager's job: Folklore and fact. *Harvard Business Review*, March–April, 163–76.

Mole, G., Plant, R. and Salaman, G. (1993) Developing executive competencies: Learning to confront, confronting to learn. *Journal of European Industrial Training*, 17(1), 3–7.

Morgan, G. (1988) *Riding the Waves of Change*. San Francisco: Jossey-Bass.

Mumford, A. (1980) *Making Experience Pay*. Maidenhead: McGraw-Hill.

Mumford, A. (1991) Individual and organisational learning. *Industrial and Commercial Training*, 23(6), 25–31.

Osbaldeston Working Party (1987) *The Making of British Managers*. London: BIM and CBI.

Pedler, M., Burgoyne, J. and Boydell, T. (1986) *A Manager's Guide to Self-Development*. Maidenhead: McGraw-Hill.

Pedler, M., Burgoyne, J. and Boydell, T. (1991) *The Learning Company*. Maidenhead: McGraw-Hill.

Peters, T. (1987) *Thriving on Chaos*. Basingstoke: Macmillan.

Peters, T. and Waterman, R. (1982) *In Search of Excellence*. New York: Harper and Row.

Pettigrew, A. (1987) Introduction: Researching strategic change, in A. Pettigrew (ed.) *The Management of Strategic Change*. Oxford: Blackwell, 1–14.

Pettigrew, A. and Whipp, R. (1991) *Managing Change for Competitive Success*. Oxford: Blackwell.

Poole, M. (1990) Editorial: Human resource management in an international perspective. *International Journal of Human Resource Management*, 1(1), 1–15.

Rackham, N., Honey, P. and Colbert, M. (1971) *Developing Interactive Skills*. Northampton: Wellens.

Roberts, J. (1992) Human resource strategies and the management of change, in *Human Resource Strategies, Supplementary Readings, 1*. Milton Keynes, Open University, 18–38.

Rogers, A. (1986) *Teaching Adults*. Milton Keynes: Open University Press.

Salaman, G. and Batsleer, J. (1994) Managing and learning, in *Managing Development and Change*, B751. Milton Keynes: Open Business School.

References

Sayles, L.R. (1964) *Managerial Behaviour*. New York: McGraw-Hill.

Schroder, H.M. (1989) *Managerial Competences*. Dubuque, IA: Kendall/ Hunt.

Senge, P. (1990) The leaders' new work. *Sloan Management Review*, 32(1), 7–23.

Sisson, K. (1990) Introducing the Human Resource Management Journal. *Human Resource Management Journal*, 1(1), 1.

Sparrow, P. and Bogdano, M. (1993) Competency requirement forecasting: Issues for international selection. *International Journal of Selection and Assessment*, 1(1), 50–8.

Steele, F. (1977) Is the culture hostile to organisation development?, in P.M. Minis and D.N. Berg (eds) *Failures in Organisation Development and Change*. New York: Wiley.

Stewart, R. (1989) Studies of managerial jobs and behaviour: The way forward. *Journal of Management Studies*, 26(1), 1–10.

Stewart, Rosemary (1967) *Managers and Their Jobs*. London: Macmillan.

Stewart, Rosemary (1983) Managerial behaviour: How research has changed the traditional picture, in M. Earl (ed.) *Perspectives on Management*. Oxford: Oxford University Press, 82–98.

Storey, J. (1992) *Developments in the Management of Human Resources*. Oxford: Blackwell.

Storey, J. and Sisson, K. (1993) *Managing Human Resources and Industrial Relations*. Buckingham: Open University Press.

Tannenbaum, R. and Schmidt, W. (1958) How to choose a leadership pattern. *Harvard Business Review*, March–April, 95–101.

Thomson, A., Pettigrew, A.M. and Rubashow, N. (1985) British management and strategic change. *European Management Journal*, 3(3), 165–73.

Thornton, G.C. and Byham, W.C. (1982) *Assessment Centres and Managerial Performance*. New York: Academic Press.

Weick, K.E. (1983) Managerial thought in the context of action, in S. Srivastva *The Executive Mind*. San Francisco, Jossey-Bass, 221–42.

Wilensky, H. (1967) *Organisational Intelligence*. New York: Basic Books.

Wilensky, J. and Wilensky, H. (1951) Personnel counselling: The Hawthorne case. *American Journal of Sociology*, LVII, November, 265–80.

Willmott, H. (1984) Images and ideals of managerial work. *Journal of Management Studies*, 21(3), 349–68.

Woodruffe, C. (1992) What is meant by a competency?, in R. Boam and P. Sparrow (eds) *Designing and Achieving Competency*. Maidenhead: McGraw-Hill, 16–30.

INDEX

142

TECHNOLOGICAL CHANGE AT WORK (2nd edition)

Ian McLoughlin and Jon Clark

'Automate or liquidate' has been a popular cry in British industry. In *Technological Change at Work* Ian McLoughlin and Jon Clark focus on automation in its most pervasive contemporary guise – computing and information technologies. They draw upon and evaluate the large body of evidence – including examples from their own extensive research and the growing body of evidence from Britain – suggesting that popular views do not always reflect the complex choices and issues that arise when these technologies are introduced.

The authors present their own 'processual' framework for understanding technological change and its outcomes, and devote considerable attention to the independent influence of the technology itself. They conclude that choices are not as tightly constrained by commercial and technical imperatives as popularly believed. Nevertheless, managers and unions still have a lot to learn in devising the most effective methods of introducing and working with new technology.

This substantially revised and extended edition examines the latest research findings, critically evaluates trends towards 'flexible specialization' and 'human resource management', and places the British experience of technological change at work in a comparative context.

Reviewers' welcoming comments on the first edition included:

> . . . a masterly summary of recent academic research on the impact of information technology in the workplace
> *(Times Higher Education Supplement)*

> . . . this book will help concerned practitioners in a variety of organizational specialisms
> *(Work Research Unit News & Abstracts)*

Contents
Introduction – New technology at work – Analysing technological change at work – The management of human resources and technological change – Trade unions and technological change – New technology, work tasks and skills – New technology, job content and work organization – New technology, supervision and control – Technological change at work in comparative perspective – Conclusions – Appendix – Bibliography – Index.

304pp   0 335 19009 X (Paperback)

MANAGING CULTURE

Peter Anthony

The management of culture currently dominates the attention of the controllers of both private and public institutions. Culture is believed to provide the key to a commitment to excellence from which will follow success, survival and profit. Some of the extensive literature implies that effective management depends upon cultural management, that nothing else needs to be done.

Managing Culture examines these claims and explains why they have been made. It describes some examples of cultural change as a preliminary to the main purpose which is to present some critical questions about the case for cultural management and about the confusions that lie behind it. The book argues that there are likely to be severe practical difficulties about the control and prediction of the outcome of change in the field of culture. It goes on to suggest that there is a real danger of cultural management causing considerable organizational damage when the instigators of change programmes are easily led to believe that the changes have worked when they have not. In these circumstances, the managers of organizational culture may find that their organizations are no longer under their control: there is a divorce between their perception and reality.

The book ends positively by asserting the advantages of understanding the culture of organizations in order to have some real hope of influencing, rather than controlling, their development.

Contents

128pp   0 335 09788 X (Paperback)   0 335 09789 8 (Hardback)

LIVERPOOL
JOHN MOORES UNIVERSITY
TRUEMAN STREET LIBRARY
15-21 WEBSTER STREET
LIVERPOOL L3 2ET
TEL. 051 231 4022/4023